Contents

Introduction

The British public is still being heavily taxed into sobriety - up to five times more than anywhere else in Europe. Worse still, duty free is due for abolition in July 1999! Combine this with a favourable exchange rate and this puts Channel Hopping high on the list of favourite British shopping and leisure pursuits.

Drinkers and smokers would do well to stock up on alcohol and tobacco, but everyone else can benefit too: for example did you know that items such as mustard, pasta and water are at least 25% less than in the UK?

And it's not just food, some makes of pots and pans, for example Tefal and Le Creuset, are half the price in France and huge savings can be made on a variety of hardware and garden products. We at the Channel Hopper's Guide have done all the legwork for you, so you'll know exactly where to go and what is worthwhile to buy, which means you'll be buying the best products at the best prices.

And if you're staying for a night or two, we have even made some hotel suggestions. But best of all, we have negotiated lots of exclusive special offers available only to you our readers, making your cross-Channel trip even better value for money!

So, whether you are looking to buy beer, cater for a special party or stock up on your favourite tipples on your way home from your Continental holiday, make sure to keep the Channel Hopper's Guide with you. Just slip it into your passport wallet. You'll find, conveniently, it's exactly the same size.

Bon Voyage....

Written By:	Sharron Livingston
Research Assistant:	Shaun M. I. Livingston
Published By:	Passport Guide Publications
Enquiries :	0181 905 4851

Special thanks to Andrew Jefford,
Wine Writer for The Evening Standard,
for his contribution to
The Channel Hopper's Guide wine tasting

Cover design, map illustrations
Michael Abrahams, Alographics
Tel: 0181 922 7242

ISBN: 0 9524319 5 5
© 1998 by Passport Guide Publications
PO Box 336, Edgware, Middx HA8 8NL

Contents

Award Winning Value!

Up to 50% Off UK High Street Prices on Duty Free*

Eurtounnel Duty Free has just been awarded the Channel Hopper's Best Value Cross Channel Duty Free Award. To celebrate we have reduced our prices even further and now offer up to 50% off UK High Street prices on selected Duty Free products. If you want to take advantage telephone *0990 35 35 35* and book yourself a ticket - *then shop 'til you drop!*

* Savings are off notional UK High Street prices for a comparable quantity, taking the average price established in a survey which is available on request. All offers are subject to availability and close at midnight (local time) 31/12/98.

EUROTUNNEL *The Fast Track to Great Savings*

Hopping Over

Cross-Channel hopping has become a familiar aspect of British life with four companies all vying for custom. See the Hopping Over table on page 8 for the options.

The cost of cross-Channel travel is still competitive with deals offered throughout the year, and this is expected to continue past abolition of duty free. It makes good sense to shop around before you travel or better still, delegate this by becoming a member of a travel club.

Travel clubs exist to put together competitive travel packages and deals and will always offer the most competitive cross-Channel fares available.

Try EuroSave Travel Club, The Ferry Travel Club or Ferry Savers all of whom are listed on these pages.

Hopping Over

One of the current perks of travelling is the opportunity to buy products at duty free prices. Whoever you buy from, you are bound to make substantial savings. Our research shows that overall Eurotunnel offer the best value cross-Channel Duty Free.

Crossing	From/To	Journey Time	Frequency
P&O Stena Line Tel: 0990 980980 Complimentary Bus service to Calais town centre	Dover/Calais Check-in: 20 mins	75 mins	Every 45 mins peak time
Hoverspeed: Hovercraft Tel: 01304 240 241 Bus service to Railway Station. Fare: 50p	Dover/Calais Check-in: 20 mins	35 mins	Every hour peak time
Hoverspeed: Seacat Tel: 01304 240 241	Folkestone/ Boulogne Check-in: 30 mins	55 mins	Hourly peak time
AWARDED BEST VALUE CROSS-CHANNEL DUTY FREE			
Le Shuttle: Tel: 0990 353535 No foot passengers. Vehicles only.	Folkestone/ Calais Turn up & go Check-in: 20 mins	35 mins	Every 15 mins peak time
SeaFrance: Tel: 0990 711711 Complimentary bus service to Calais Town Centre	Dover/ Calais Check-in: 30 mins	90 mins	Every 90 mins peak time

Channel Travel Radio

More of the information you need as you travel to France.

As you drive along the M20, head towards your ferry or prepare to board your shuttle, be sure to tune in to Channel Travel Radio. 107.6FM is the frequency to find if you want to hear all the very latest cross-Channel travel information.

Channel Travel Radio broadcasts live, 24 hours a day from Eurotunnel's control centre in Folkestone. Tune in and you'll hear up-to-the-minute shuttle and ferry departure information, the latest continental weather forecasts and news about the conditions on Europe's roads. There are also lots of ideas on places to visit and things to do while you're abroad as well as a great selection of music.

If you'd like a special request on the station, you can write to Channel Travel Radio, PO Box 2000, Folkestone, Kent CT18 8XY or call 01303 283823.

Focus on Folkestone

With the advent of the Chunnel Tunnel Folkestone has become a throughway for travellers to and from the Continent. So what does Folkestone have to offer?

This elegant town has an old harbour, a busy fishing fleet, and the pretty Leas Promenade. The mile long promenade is the setting for the free Shepway Festival Airshow and also the Bandstand.

Just five miles from Folkestone, amidst charming countryside is Westhanger - the home for Kent's only racecourse. Westhanger Station is conveniently located nearby.

Golf in Folkestone is popular. The most established course in Folkestone, Littlestone, was used as a qualifier for the British Open.

The coast from Dungeness to Folkestone and beyond the Goodwin Sands offers the best sea fishing in the U.K. and this is the venue for the European and All England Sea Angling Championships which are held annually. Freshwater anglers can enjoy the secluded lake in Brockhill Country Park near Hythe or along the leafy banks of the Royal Military Canal.

Folkestone also has much to offer the would-be shopper. The sprawling seafront market is the South East's biggest, and is an Aladdin's cave for bargain hunters. Sandgate is a leading antiques centre, as is Hythe, with its charming Olde Worlde high street and shops.

Whilst in Folkestone you can visit the Rotunda amusement park. There are 17 types of rides and go-karting. It also has its own Sunday market which, with over 200 stalls, is an ideal place to find a bargain!

A relaxing walk along Folkestone Harbour will reward you with a regional variety of freshly caught seafood which will warm the cockles of your heart!

Tourist Information Centre
Harbour Street, Folkestone
CT20 1QN
Tel: 01303 258594.

Focus on Dover

*Crossing the Channel from
Dover to Calais is
now traditional for the Brits. So much
so that we no longer notice the
White Cliffs on our way out !*

As you drive or even sail into the port of Dover, you cannot help but be overwhelmed by the towering stature of the celebrated White Cliffs. If you venture higher to the east of Dover you will find yourself on The Langdon Cliffs which is part of the National Trust parkland. Here you can follow the cliff top trails and enjoy the stunning views across the Channel.

The Cliffs are also home to Dover Castle, described as 'The Key of England'. Visit the secret balcony high up inside the White Cliffs where Winston Churchill watched part of the Battle of Britain. Close by you can see the Roman Lighthouse, built to serve as a guiding light for ships entering the harbour. On the opposite side of Dover Castle are The Western Heights home to fortifications, trenches and ramparts which were built in the 16th and 17th centuries.

A major attraction at Dover is the White Cliffs Experience.

With the aid of films and recreations you can see archaeological remains. You will discover historical Britain from the time of Julius Ceasar through to the Roman Conquest, Saxon and Viking Ages right up to the 1940s and World War II. Dover's own colourful history starting from prehistoric times, is also highlighted.

Turning one's attention to one of Dover's more relaxing venues; log fires, beer gardens and live music are all images that instantly spring to mind. Dover's traditional Kentish style pub culture is very popular and is an ideal way to enjoy an informal evening's entertainment perhaps with a pint or two with dinner.

Tourist Information Centre
Townall Street, Dover
Tel: 01304 205108

The White Cliffs Experience
Market Square, Dover
Tel: 01304 214566

How Much Can You Bring Back?

Go Ahead - stock up.
But do not go over the top. If your purchases exceed the Advisory Guidelines, as set by customes and excise, you could be stopped!

Since 1st January 1993, you are permitted to bring back as much alcohol and tobacco as you like, but it must be for personal use only. So you can happily stock up for Christmas or parties or weddings.

Although H. M. Customs and Excise have no authority to limit the amount you bring back into this country they do have the right to stop you if your purchases exceed the 'Advisory Guidelines'. In this case you may be required to prove that the goods are for your own personal use.

If you are stopped, remember that the H.M. Customs officer is looking for bootleggers or those intent on resale and your co-operation will be appreciated. Other products such as mineral water, or any other non-alcoholic or food products are not limited in any way. Enjoy.

Advisory Guidelines
as set by H.M. Customs & Excise

Wine (not to exceed 60 litres of sparkling wine)	90 litres
Spirits	10 litres
Intermediate products (i.e port & sherry)	20 litres
Beer	100 litres
Cigarettes	800
Cigars	400
Tobacco	1 Kilogram

Out and About in France

*A few essential tips to make your
bargain-hunting
travels a little easier ...
and perhaps a little cheaper.*

En Route:
To comply with French motoring regulations, please note what is and is not essential:

It is essential:
• To have a full UK driving licence and all motoring documents.
• To be over the age of 18 - even if you have passed your test in the UK.
• Not to exceed 90km/h in the first year after passing your test.
• To display a GB sticker.
• To carry a warning triangle.
• To wear rear seat belts if fitted.
• To affix headlamp diverters. These are widely available in motoring shops or DIY with black masking tape.

It is not essential to:
• Arrange a green card from your insurance company for France.
• Have yellow headlights.

Motorways & Roads:
French motorways (autoroutes) are marked by blue and white 'A' signs. Many motorways are privately owned and outside towns a toll charge (péage) is usually payable and can be expensive. This can be paid by credit card (Visa Card, Eurocard, Mastercard), cash or even coins at automatic gates so be prepared. Contact a tourist board or information centre on the motorway network to find out the exact cost. Incidentally, the Calais to Boulogne motorway is toll free.

Other roads are as follows:
'D roads - routes départementales - the scenic alternatives to 'A' roads.
C roads - routes communales - country roads.
'N Roads - routes nationales - toll free, single lane roads. Slower than 'A' roads.

**IMPORTANT! DRIVE ON THE RIGHT,
OVERTAKE ON THE LEFT**

Out and About in France

Breakdown on Motorways:
If you should be unlucky enough to breakdown on the motorway and you do not have breakdown cover, DON'T PANIC you can still get assistance.

There are emergency telephones stationed every mile and a half on the motorway. These are directly linked to the local Police Station. The Police will be able to automatically locate you and arrange for an approved repair service to come to your aid. Naturally there is a cost for this and fees are regulated. Expect to pay around £50 for servicing plus the cost of parts and around £55 for towing.
An extra 25% supplement is also charged if you break down between 6pm and 8am and any time on Saturdays, Sundays and national holidays!
At the garage, ensure you ask for un Ordre de Réparation (repair quote) which you should sign. This specifies the exact nature of the repairs, how long it will take to repair your vehicle and, most importantly, the cost!

Emergency Phrases:

Please, help
Aidez-moi s'il vous plaît

My car has broken down
Ma voiture est en panne

I have run out of petrol
Je suis en panne d'essence

The engine is overheating
Le moteur surchauffe

There is a problem with the brakes
Il y a un problème de freins

I have a flat tyre
J'ai un pneu crevé

The battery is flat
La batterie est vide

There is a leak in the petrol tank/in the radiator
Il y a une fuite dans le réservoir d'essence/dans le radiateur

Can you send a mechanic/breakdown van?
Pouvez vous envoyer un mécanicien/une dépanneuse?

Can you tow me to a garage?
Pouvez-vous me remorquer jusqu'à un garage?

I have had an accident
J'ai eu un accident

The windscreen is shattered
Le pare-brise est cassé

Call an ambulance
Appelez une ambulance

Out and About in France

Speed Limits:
In France speed limits are shown in kilometres per hour not miles per hour. Always adhere to these speed limits as in France they are strictly enforced:

	MPH	km/h
Toll motorways	81	130
Dual Carriageways	69	110
Other Roads	55	90
Towns	31	50

When raining, these speed limits are reduced by 6mph on the roads and 12mph on the motorway. In fog, speed is restricted to 31mph. As well as speed traps, it is useful to know that entrance and exit times through the toll booths can be checked on your toll ticket and may be used as evidence of speeding!

Roadside Messages:
For safety's sake, it is very important to be aware of the following roadside messages:

Carrefour	Crossroad
Déviation	Diversion
Priorité à droite	

Give way to traffic on the right

Péage	Toll
Vous n'avez pas la priorité	Give way
Ralentir	Slow down
Rappel	Restriction continues
Sens unique	One way
Serrez à droite/ à gauche	Keep right/ left
Véhicules lents	Slow vehicles

Other messages:

Gravillons	Loose chippings
Chaussée Déformée	Uneven road & temporary surface
Nids de Poules	Potholes

Tyre Pressure:
It is crucial to ensure that your tyres are at the correct pressure to cater for heavy loads. Make sure you do not exceed the car's maximum carrying weight.

The following table gives a guide to how heavy typical loads are:

1 case of	Qty	Weight kg	lbs
Wine	x 2	15kg	33lbs
Champagne	x12	22kg	48lbs
Beer 25cl	x 2	8kg	18lbs

Out and About in France

Drink Driving:
UK drink/drive laws are mild at 80mg alcohol, compared to France. French law dictates that a 50g limit of alcohol is allowed - just 1 glass of wine. Exceeding this limit risks confiscation of your licence and an on-the-spot fine of anything between 200FF (£25) to 30,000FF (almost £4,000!)

Parking For Less:
Illegal parking in France can be penalised by a fine, wheel clamping or vehicle removal. Park wherever you see a white dotted line or if there are no markings at all. There are also numerous 'pay and display' parking meters. In Calais (not Boulogne), the good news is that these parking meters take English 10p, 20p & 50p coins. The French Franc coins they take are FF1, FF2 and FF5 which roughly equate to 11p, 22p & 55p making it slightly cheaper to use your English coins - *well, every little helps!*

Filling Up:
To fill up, head for petrol stations attached to the hypermarkets (i.e. Auchan, Continent, PG Intermarché) as these usually offer the best value fuel. Though sterling is not accepted, credit cards usually are. Some petrol stations have automated payment facilities by credit card. These are generally 24 hour petrol stations and tend to be unmanned in the evening. Currently fuel is cheaper in France - diesel especially. Petrol grades are as follows

Unleaded petrol - l'essence sans plomb. Available in 95 & 98 grades - equates to UK premium and super grades respectively.

Leaded petrol - l'essence or Super Graded as 90 octane (2 star), 93 octane (3 star) & 97 octane (4 star).

Gazole - Diesel Fuel

GPL - LPG (liquefied petroleum gas)

Good News About Car Fuel
Elf, the French-owned petrol station has recently launched their **Optane Evolution**. Their petrol has been fortified with additives resulting in 3 great benefits:
1. An extra 30km on your journey per tankful.
2. Petrol smells great. Amazing but true their petrol is an in-car air freshener!
3. 25% less emissions.

Elf is the first petrol station from the Channel tunnel. It is the first place you are able stop, spend a penny or grab a bite. Show your guide and get a free cup of coffee. There's also a travel shop.

Out and About in France

Traffic News:
Tune in to Autoroute FM107.7 for French traffic news in English and French.

Phoning Home:
Phonecards (Télécartes) are widely used and available at travel centres, post offices, tobacconists and shops displaying the Télécarte sign. Coin operated payphones (becoming rare) take 1,2 & 5 FF coins. Cheap rate (50% extra time) is between 22.30hrs-08.00hrs Monday to Friday, 14.00hrs-08.00hrs Saturday, all day Sunday & public holidays. To call the UK dial 00, at the dialling tone dial 44 followed by the phone number omitting 0 from the STD code.

Writing Home:
Post Offices (PTT) are open Monday to Friday during office hours and half day on Saturday. Stamps can also be purchased from tobacconists. The cost of a postcard home is FF2.80. The small but bright yellow post boxes are easy to spot.

Tourist Offices:
- Office du Tourisme or Syndicat d'initiative:
Calais Tourist Office is at 12 Boulevard Clemenceau opposite the train station
Tel: (00 33) 321 96 62 40

Boulogne Tourist Office is at Quai de la Poste
Tel: (00 33) 321 31 68 38
They are closed 12.30-2pm)

Taxi!
It is cheaper to hail a taxi in the street or look for cab ranks indicated by the letter 'T' rather than order one by telephone. This is because a telephone requested taxi will charge for the time taken to reach you. Taxi charges are regulated. The meter must show the minimum rate on departure and the total amount (tax included) on arrival. If the taxi driver agrees that you share the taxi ride, he has the right to turn the meter back to zero at each stop showing the minimum charge again. A tip *(pourboire)* is expected. It is customary to pay 10-15%.

Currency:
French currency, known as the French Franc is shown in 3 ways: FF, Fr or F. A Franc, roughly equivalent to 11p, is made up of 100 centimes. Centimes have their own set of coins *(pièces)* i.e. 5, 10, 20 and 50 centimes - marked as 1/2F. Francs 1, 2, 5, 10 and 20F coins and bank notes *(billets)* are in 20, 50, 100, 200 and 500F notes. As of January 1st 1999 the Euro will also be legal tender though not yet circulated.

Out and About in France

Caught on the Hop!

Cafés generally allow you to use their toilets for free. In shopping complexes you may require a 1FF coin to gain entry. If you see a white saucer, place a coin or two in it. In the streets you may come across the Sanisette, a white cylindrical shaped building. Insert 2FF in the slot to open the door. After use the Sanisette completely scrubs and polishes itself.

Money Matters:

Changing money from Sterling to French Francs tends to be expensive. We recommend that you use your credit card as credit card companies give a better rate of exchange and do not charge commission when buying goods abroad. Of course you will require some cash. Change your money in the UK where it can be a little more competitive than in France. In France you can also change money and cash travellers cheques at the Post Office (PTT), banks, stations and private bureaux de change. In hypermarket complexes there are machines available to change your Sterling to French Francs. AVOID these as they are the most expensive method for changing money. It would be better to make a purchase in

the hypermarket in Sterling, as change is given in French Francs without commission charges. Although convenient, be aware of the exchange rate.

Shopping by Credit Card:

To use your credit card ensure that you have your passport handy as you may be expected to produce it.

Shopping:

Supermarket trolleys (les chariots) require a (refundable) 10 franc piece. Keep one handy to avoid queuing for change.

Public Holidays:

Most French shops will be shut on the following days

Jan 1	New Year	Jour de l'an
Apr*	Easter Monday	Lundi de Pâques
May 1	Labour Day	Fête du Travail
May 8	Victory Day	Armistice 1945
May*	Ascension	Ascension
May*	Whitsun	Lundi de Pentecôte
July 14	Bastille Day	Fête nationale
Aug 15	Assumption	Assomption
Nov 1	All Saints'	Toussaint
Nov 11	Armistice Day	Armistice 1918
Dec 25	Christmas	Noël

*Dates change each year.

No Smoking!

The French have an etiquette for everything including smoking. It is forbidden to smoke in public places. There are quite often spaces reserved in cafés and restaurants for smokers!

Out and About in France

General Conversions:

What's Your Size?
When buying clothes in France, check the conversion tables below to find out your size:

Women's Shoes

GB		FR	GB		FR
3	=	35½	5½	=	39
3½	=	36	6	=	39½
4	=	37	6½	=	40
4½	=	37½	7	=	40½
5	=	38	8	=	41½

Women's Clothing

GB		FR	GB		FR
8	=	34	14	=	40
10	=	36	16	=	42
12	=	38	18	=	44

Men's Shirts

GB		FR	GB		FR
14½	=	37	16	=	41
15	=	38	16½	=	42
15½	=	39/40	17	=	43

Men's Suits

GB		FR	GB		FR
36	=	46	42	=	52
38	=	48	44	=	54
40	=	50	46	=	56

Men's Shoes

GB		FR	GB		FR
8	=	42	9½	=	44
8½	=	43	10½	=	45

What's The Time?

Central European Time (Greenwich Mean Time + 1 hour in winter and + 2 hours in Summer) is followed in France. This means that most of the time France is one hour ahead. The clocks are put forward 1 hour in the spring and put back 1 hour in the autumn.

Passports:

Before travelling to France ensure you have a full passport.

Electricity:

If you wish to use any electrical appliances from the UK, you will need a Continental adapter plug (with round pins). The voltage in France is 220V similar to 240V in the UK.

Another important difference is that the French standard TV broadcast system is SECAM whereas in the UK it is PAL. This means that French video tapes cannot be played on English videos.

Weights and Measures:

Distance 1.6 km=	1 mile
Weight 1 kg	=	2.20lbs
Liquid 4.54 litres=	1 gallon
Liquid 1 litre	=	1.76 pints
Length 1m	=	39.37inches
Area 1sq metre	=	1.196 sq yds

A Channel Shopper's Guide

Everyone knows that alcohol is cheaper to buy in France. But beware, not everything is a bargain! Included within these pages are the outlets we consider to be the best in Calais and Bolougne. We have also highlighted other information such as whether free wine tasting *(dégustation)* is available, accepted payment methods, and, importantly, opening times.

There seems to be a lot of competition, but take a closer look - there are differences. Some outlets specialise in bargain basement wines with a 'pile 'em high sell 'em cheap' policy, but offer little in the way of service. Others are little more expensive but have a less frantic turnover of products allowing time for tasting and personal service.

We have included an appraisal of the outlets with wine recommendations and a listing of sparkling wine and beer together with a guide to prices. An extensive wine listing for each outlet would be impossible due to the sheer variety (two outlets have over 1000 wines in stock!). However, it is important to be aware that the more expensive the wine, the less the saving. ***Champagne is a notable exception - expect to pay half UK prices in France!*** Otherwise UK duty is influenced by the alcoholic content. The rate of duty remains constant regardless of quality or price range. Take a bottle of wine starting life at £1.00: a typical price breakdown once on British shores is as follows:

Cost of wine	£1.00
Duty & VAT	£1.42
Shipping	£0.17
Retailer's Profit 30%	£0.78
Total cost	£3.37

The duty on a bottle of champagne is £1.50 and on a bottle of sherry is £1.40. An average saving of £1.50 on wine under £10 makes the purchase relatively cheap. More expensive wines attract higher percentages of profit leaving little room for savings - if any! As prices constantly fluctuate because of market forces and exchange rates we aim to serve only as a guide. All currency conversions shown are at a rate FF9.4 to £1.00 but check the prevailing exchange rate.

Calais Town

Calais is the closest French port to England and the evident touristic appeal centres around shopping. But is that all Calais has to offer?

Having suffered the ravages of war, Calais was completely rebuilt after World War II. Most people now see this port as a lattice-work of commercial streets, conveniently located solely to enjoy the benefits of cheaper shopping. Right?

Well, maybe not. Its well established cross-Channel links and its geographical location makes it a good starting point to many destinations. The motorway network via the A26 and A16 means easy journies to Belgium, Strasbourg, Paris, Germany and the rest of France. Aside from its commercial centre, the Calais area has a good range of leisure activities. The vast sandy beaches offer sailing, sail boarding, speed sailing, sand yachting or just plain sun bathing. Surrounding the area is beautiful countryside where you can take a leisurely stroll or ramble over cliffs, woods and hills. Alternatively, you can go off-road cycling, horse riding and even fishing.

Along the Opal Coast, the dramatic landscape is inviting. At the Cap Blanc-Nez you will find chalk cliffs, dunes and rocks. The high ground here affords some panoramic views across the Channel. Further along is the picturesque coastline of Cap Gris-Nez with its fishing villages. You can spend a weekend just visiting the resorts and fishing ports. The area between the two Caps is known as 'le site des deux caps' and provides an attractive environment in which to spend a delightful weekend away.

There is also much to appeal to the nature lover. The Regional Nature Park, 'L'Audomarois' in St Omer, offers nature trails to explore the environment. It has been well preserved and the nature paths are well signposted. These trails can be made on foot, horseback or by bike. Guided tours are also available.

Golfing facilities around Calais are becoming ever more popular. If this is your sport then you will be pleased to know that there are three 18 hole golf courses nearby in Wimereux, St. Antoine and St. Omer.

And if all this is too much, you can always take one of the canal cruises along the waterways that criss-cross the Marais Audomarois and contemplate your next shopping trip!

Canal Cruises
Cruises with commentary which last 45-90 mins. Pont de la Guillotine, Rivage de Tilques (near St Omer). Call in advance Tel 00 33 321 95 10 19.

Cycle Hire
178 boulevard la Fayette. Mountain bikes (VTTs) from FF100 Location VTT Brame Sports

Golf Golf du Bois de Rumingham - 18 holes 1613 rue St-Antoine (20km south-east of Calais) off the N43. Tel: 00 33 321 85 30 33.

Golf d'Aa-St. Omer
9 and 18 holes chemin des Bois, Acquin-Westbécourt Tel: 00 33 321 38 59 90.

Golf de Wimereux - 18 holes route d'Ambleteuse, Wimereux Tel: 00 33 321 32 43 20.

Marais Audomarois
Fishing, rowing boats, boat trips & canal ('watergang') cruises Regional Nature Park Audomarois Tel: 00 33 321 98 62 98 La Grange Nature de Claimarais Tel: 00 33 321 95 23 40

Offshore Cruises
Sail down the Côte d'Opale on the yacht Ophelie to Cap Blanc-Nez Tel: 00 33 321 93 63 71 or contact the tourist office.

Riding
Escorted countryside rides contact Cheval Loisir, 182 route de Gravelines, Calais Tel:00 33 321 9718 18

General Market Days
Place de Crève coeur (map ref: D4/5) All day Thursday & Saturday a.m.

Take in a few sights while in Calais. After all it was under English rule for more than 200 years during the Occupation of 1347-1558.

Hôtel de Ville, place du Soldat Inconnu

One of Calais' finest land-marks is the town hall which can be seen for miles around. This magnificent Flemish- style structure was completed in 1925 and dominates the main square. It houses many paintings and is adorned with stained glass windows. The interior is renowned for the elaborate decor of the reception rooms. Also attached to the town hall is an ornate brick clock tower.

Eglise Notre-Dame, rue Notre Dame

In 1921 General de Gaulle married a local girl called Yvonne Vendroux here. The architecture is partly English Gothic in style, perhaps because it dates back to before and during the English occupation.

The Town Hall. Inset : Rodin's Burghers

Les Six Bourgeois de Calais

Citadelle
nr Square Vauban

This was originally built to house the town's garrison after the French retook Calais and dates back to 1560. In the 17th century much of the later work is attributable to the French engineer Vauban. These days it is partly used as a sports centre.

Musée de la Guerre
parc St. Pierre

The war museum is open daily from 10am-5pm from February to December. Entrance fee is FF15 (children FF10). This camouflaged bunker is situated opposite the town hall in an old German bunker. It served as a telephone exchange during the second World War. You approach it via a walk through the Parc St Pierre.

Musée de Beaux Arts et
de la Dentelle, rue Richelieu

The museum is open Wednesday to Monday 10am-noon & 2-5.30pm. Entry is FF10 (kids free).

It houses paintings from 15th to 20th centuries and sculpture from 19th & 20th centuries. Also on display are exhibits from Calais' lace industry - an industry originally imported from England.

Rodin's Six Burghers
place du Soldat Inconnu

At the foot of the clock tower and Town Hall stands Rodin's original 19th century bronze statue of The Burghers of Calais. The statue recalls the final year of the Hundred Years War when the mayor, with other prominent citizens assembled here, wearing only their shirts, before surrendering to King Edward. They were willing to sacrifice their lives to save Calais from being massacred by King Edward II at the end of his 6 month siege. Their heroism moved the King's French wife, Philippine, to successfully plead for their pardon.

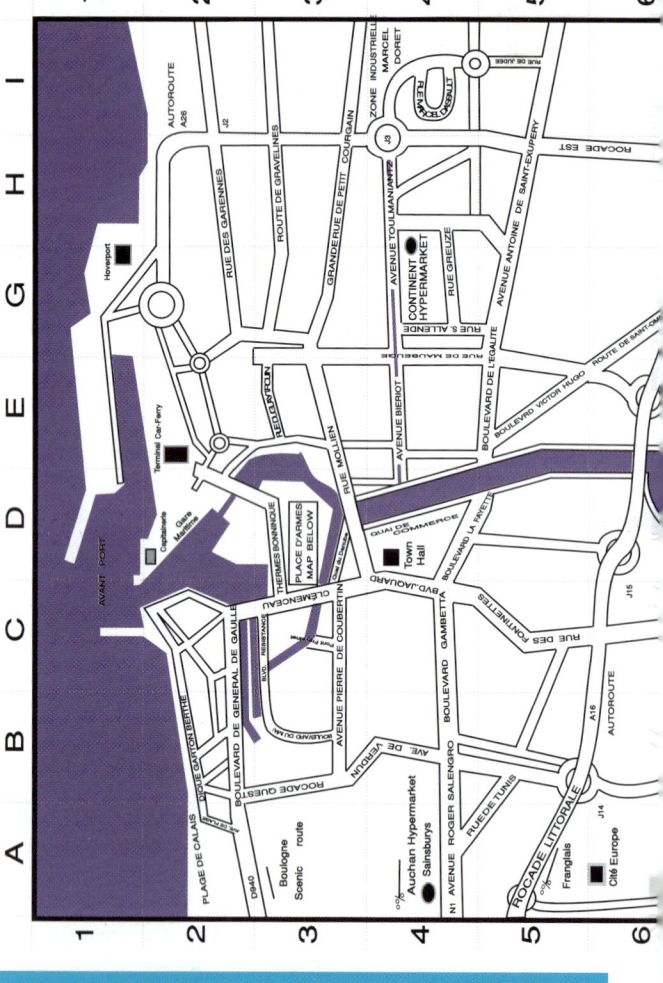

Expanded Map Below of PLACE D'ARMES

QUAI FOURNIER
RUE DE OSTENDE
RUE DE BAILLON
RUE DE CONSTAD
RUE DE MOSCOU
RUE DE RIGA
PLACE D'ANGLETERRE
PLACE DE LORRAINE
RUE DE HOLIANDE
RUE DE METZ
PLACE DE NORVEGE
RUE DE LONDRES
RUE DE LISBONNE
RUE DE MADRID
RUE BERTHOIS
C. DUPONT
COTE. DOMINIQUE
RUE DES PRETRES
RUE ST. PIERRE
PLACE DE RUE NOTRE-DAME
RUE DES MARECHAUX
CHARCOT
RUE DE THERMES
PLACE DE RHEIMS
DE GOURDON
RUE BENNITES
RUE SEIGN
RUE FERNLENEL
RUE GAVE DES AILES
BOULEVARD DES ALLIES
RUE DEBOUT
PLACE D'ARMES
RUE DE LA PAIS
RUE TOMSOUVILLE
RUE RAVISSE MARCHE
PL. DU PETIT CORRE
RUE DE HAVRE
R. A. GERSCHELL
RUE ROYALE

Saint Omer
LeChai Ardresien
N43
SOUTH
COQUELLES
Le Shuttle

Aldi Supermarket
Rue Mollien
Calais

Map Ref: E3
Bus No: 2
English: No
Tasting: No
Payment: Cash only. Sterling
           accepted but the
           exchange rate is low.
Parking: Yes
Open: Mon-Sat 9am-7pm,
Closed: Mon-Fri 12-2pm/Sun

How To Get There

From the ferry terminal follow signs to Centre Ville. At the roundabout take the second exit marked Centre Ville. Continue (railway on the right). At the end turn left into Rue Mollien. Aldi is 100 yards along on the right hand side in an inlet.

On the surface, this looks like a very down market supermarket - and so it is. Yet among the outrageously bad wines there are one or two redeeming features.

 ★ STAR BUYS ★

Fitou, £1.50
Deep colour, light & smooth
Côtes du Roussillon, £1.00
Its ripe currant fruit makes it a very quaffable steal.

Crémant d'Alsace £2.70 This sparkler goes down very well at parties.

Aldi also sell a great tasting pale ale which is ideal for parties: Maître Brasseur Blonde 4.7%. At just 13p per 25cl bottle this must merit some space in your car boot.

Incidentally, for parties, this is the best place to buy crisps, nuts, olives, and

What's On Offer At Aldi?

Quantities 75cl unless otherwise shown. Prices in-store are in French Francs (FF) converted to Sterling (£) for your convenience at a rate FF9.40 to £1.00.

Sparkling wine	% Vol	FF	£
Crémant de Limoux		19.95	2.12
Crémant d'Alsace		21.95	2.33
Beer	**% Vol**	**FF**	**£**
Kusterbier 10 x 25cl	4.7	12.95	1.37
Ecu D'Or 6 x25cl	6.4	13.95	1.48
Special Upper 6 X 25cl	7.5	13.95	1.48
Brune Terken 6 x 25cl	6.7	14.95	1.59
Maître Brasseur Blonde 24 x 25cl	4.7	28.45	3.02

Auchan Hypermarket

AUCHAN HYPERMARKET
Fort Nieulay, Route de Boulogne (RN1)

Map Ref: A4
Bus No: 5
English: Yes
Tasting: Promotion wines only
Payment: £, 💳 💳
Parking: Yes
Open: Monday to Saturday
           8.30am-10pm
Closed: Sunday

BEST CROSS-CHANNEL HYPERMARKET GROUP

Auchan Hypermarket, once known as Mammouth, has seen vast improvements instore. The layout makes for easy shopping. It is brightly lit, colourful, and spacious. The vast range of wines come from major French regions with a nod from Portugal, Morroco and Spain.

There is also an array of popular Champagnes, beers and spirits which seem competitively priced.

⭐ STAR BUYS ⭐

1996 Fitou Tradition Roc Flamboyant, FF20.96/£1.98
Hot and hard but with some Southern French tang.

How to Get There

From the ferry terminal take the motorway following the signs for Boulogne and exit at Junction (sortie) 14 just follow signs for Coquelles or Auchan. From Le Shuttle cross the roundabout following signs for Calais and then follow signs for Coquelles or Auchan.

1996 Château Lalands, St Julien, FF67.16/£7.14
Deep in colour with a light cedar bouquet. Chewy, thick and soft textured with spicy, earthy fruit to taste

1996 Sauternes Pierre Chanau , FF67.96/£7.22
The bottle betrays the contents - scents of gentle pollen, soft, sweet and honeyed. A great sweet wine for sipping.

Veuve Emile Grande Réserve Champagne FF79.97/£8.48
A good basic Champagne, with some yeasty complexities beneath its apple incision.

Auchan also have wine in a 1-litre carton, Carré de Vigne Tetra Brik, Vin de Table de France at around 93p. Although a little thin

it is palatable enough at the price. Another in this style is Canterrane, Vin de Table Blanc, at around 66p, not great but appealing, clean, fresh and good value.

What's On Offer At Auchan?
Quantities 75cl unless otherwise shown. Prices in-store are in French Francs (FF) converted to Sterling (£) here for your convenience at a rate FF9.4 to £1.00.

Sparkling wine	FF	£
'Splendid' Dry German	9.95	1.06
Muscabur Brut & Rosé	12.80	1.36
Paul Bur Blanc de Blancs Brut	16.95	1.80
Blanquette de Limoux Demi-Sec	21.95	2.33
Charles Volner Blanc de Blancs Brut & Demi Sec	23.80	2.53
Crémant d'Alsace, J G Keller	27.95	2.97
Café de Paris Demi Sec	26.95	2.86
Kritter Demi Sec	28.50	3.03
Blanquette de Limoux Brut	28.50	3.03
Clairette de Die Brut	29.10	3.09
Saumur Ackerman Brut & Demi Sec	29.35	3.12
Aimery Blanquette de Limoux Brut	29.95	3.12
Asti, Italian	29.95	3.12
Crémant de Bourgogne Brut, Charmelion	29.95	3.12
Josep Masachs Cava, Spanish Demi Sec	29.95	3.12
Vouvray Demi Sec	29.95	3.12
Foussy Brut	30.95	3.29
Ackerman Privelege Brut	32.50	3.45
Saumur Gratien & Meyer Brut	33.50	3.56
Crémant de Loire Brut, Comte de Montmorency	34.95	3.71
Crémant de Alsace Brut Blanc de Noirs, Dopff	39.95	4.25
Sir James Australian Brut	46.95	4.99
Champagne	**FF**	**£**
Philippe de Nantheuil Brut	52.05	5.53
Oudinot Brut	69.95	7.44
De Reyve Brut	72.50	7.71
Nicolas Feuillate	77.70	8.24
Vranken	79.40	8.44
Veuve Emille Brut	79.90	8.50
Duval Leroy	82.50	8.77
Germain Brut	83.60	8.89
Nicolas Feuillate	85.10	9.05
Jacquart Brut	87.60	9.31
Mercier Brut	87.95	9.35

Champagne contd.	FF	£
De Castellane Brut	88.00	9.36
Alfred Rothschild & Co Brut	88.15	9.37
Charles Lafitte Brut Grand Cuvée	89.95	9.56
Jean Maire Cuvée Brut '95	90.25	9.60
Veuve Emille Blanc de Blancs Grand Cru '91	99.00	10.53
Lanson Black Label	109.75	11.67
Princess de France	114.95	12.22
Heidsiek & Co Monopole Brut	115.70	12.30
Laurent Perrier	121.40	12.91
Mumm Cordon Rouge Brut	123.65	13.15
Veuve Clicquot Ponsardin	134.95	14.35
Demoiselle	139.95	14.88
Moët Chandon 1er Cru	145.00	15.42
Moët Chandon Dry Imperial	149.95	15.95

Beers	% Vol	FF	£
Helbrau 10 x 25cl	2.8	11.05	1.17
Norvilland 24 x 25cl	4.0	27.95	2.97
Sterling 24 x 25cl	4.9	36.60	3.89
Facon 24 x 25cl	4.9	39.90	4.24
St Omer 24 x 25cl	5.0	40.25	4.28
Meteor 24 x 25cl	4.6	41.95	4.46
33 Export 24 x 25cl	4.8	43.05	4.57
Kanterbrau 24 x 25cl	4.7	43.95	4.67
Pelforth Blonde 20 x 25cl	5.8	44.50	4.73
Seumeuse 24 x 25cl	5.0	45.60	4.85
Stella Artois 24 x 25cl	5.2	49.95	5.31
Spitfire 12 x 50cl	4.7	74.95	7.97
Bishop's Finger 12 x 50cl	5.4	78.50	8.35
Dempsey's 20 x 50cl (+ 4 free)	4.8	116.69	12.41
Bombardier 24 x 50cl	4.3	119.95	12.76
Amsterdam Mariner 24 x 50cl	5.0	119.95	12.76
Foster's Ice 24 x 33cl	5.0	119.95	12.76
Skona Extra 24 x 50cl	8.6	119.95	12.76
Badger Brewery 24 x 50cl	4.0	139.95	14.88
Tangle Foot 24 x 50cl	5.0	139.95	14.88
Grölsch 24 x 50cl	5.0	149.95	15.95
Carling Black Label 24 x 50cl	4.1	159.95	17.01
Old Speckled Hen 24 x 33cl	5.2	169.95	18.07
Newcastle Brown Ale 24 x 33cl	4.5	179.95	19.14
John Smith Extra 24 x 44cl	4.0	184.95	19.67
Caffrey's 24 x 50cl	4.8	189.95	20.20
Guinness Draught 24 x 44cl	4.1	219.95	23.39
Holsten Pils 24 x 44cl	5.5	219.95	23.39

Carrefour Hypermarket
Cité Europe
Coquelles

Map Ref:	A6
Bus No:	7
English:	No
Tasting:	No
Payment:	£, Eurocheques, VISA ●
Parking:	Yes
Open:	Monday to Friday 9am-10pm Saturday 8.30am-10pm
Closed:	Sunday

How To Get There

From Calais port turn left onto the A26. Follow the road signposted Dunkerque onto A16. Exit junction (sortie) 18, follow signs to Boulogne. Exit at junction (sortie) 12 signposted Cité Europe Ouest. Follow signs to Cité de la Europe, Centre Commercial. You will soon see Cité Europe. Carrefour is on the right (or left depending on where you park) as you enter.

Carrefour hypermarket is a giant dominating the mouth of Cité Europe. It is brightly lit, well laid out, colourful and huge. So huge that some of the staff get around on roller skates!

Unfortunately Carrefour did not take part in our wine tasting this year, so we are unable to bring you any recommendations.

At one end of the hypermarket are the quality French wines and champagnes, beautifully displayed. For some reason all the other wines are displayed at the other end of the hypermarket. Interestingly, that includes wines from other parts of the world. At this end there is also an array of popular sparkling wines, a varied range of beers and a formidable range of spirits.

Their beers include popular Belgium Trappiste beers including Satan Gold, 8% (3 x 33cl FF35.20/£3.74) - buy it and you become eligible to join the Satan Beer Supporters Club! The shelves include two 12% ABV heavyweights; one from Germany - EKU 28 - (3 x 33cl, FF26.10/ £2.77) reputed to have the highest gravity of any bottom-fermenting beer in the world! And a native beer - La Bière du Demon - (3 x 33cl 24.75FF/ £2.63) a French pale ale with the inscription '*12% de Plaisir Diabolique*' on its label.

What's On Offer At Carrefour?
Quantities 75cl unless otherwise shown. Prices in-store are in French Francs (FF) converted to Sterling (£) here for your convenience at a rate FF9.40 to £1.00.

Sparkling wine	FF	£
Impérial Regent Demi Sec	6.25	0.66
Musacador Blanc Doux (sweet) & Rosé	10.50	1.11
J. Heiffer Blanc de Blancs Brut & Demi Sec	16.50	1.75
Moscato Spumante	19.30	2.05
Blue Nun Sparkling	19.95	2.12
Charles Volner Brut	23.65	2.51
Saumur Demi Sec	24.80	2.63
Asti	25.05	2.66
Crémant d'Alsace Brut	25.40	2.70
Blanquette de Limoux Brut &Demi Sec	25.80	2.74
Crémant de Bourgogne	25.90	2.75
Café de Paris Demi Sec	26.95	2.86
Opéra Demi Sec	28.60	3.04
Kritter Brut de Brut & Demi Sec	28.65	3.04
Saumur Ackerman Demi Sec	29.20	3.10
Clairette de Die Brut	29.25	3.10
Clairette de Die Tradition	30.55	3.25
Louis de Vernier Blanc de Blancs	31.00	3.29
Cava Verier Semi Seco	31.00	3.29
Saumur Cuvée Cassandre	34.90	3.71
Vouvray Ackerman Brut	39.50	4.20
Ackerman Privilege Crémant de Loire	39.95	4.25
Champagne	FF	£
Louis Rozier 1er Cru	59.60	6.34
De Staël	73.50	7.81
Charles de Cazenove	74.20	7.89
Paul George Brut Tradition	79.00	8.40
Vranken Brut	79.40	8.44
Hubert de Claminger	80.00	8.51
Germain Demi Sec	81.70	8.69
Nicolas Feuillatte	82.20	8.74
Mercier Demi Sec	87.95	9.35
Alfred Rothschild Brut	88.75	9.44
Binet Brut	89.00	9.46
Mercier Brut Rosé	95.85	10.19

Carrefour Hypermarket

Champagne contd.	FF	£
Canard Duchêne Brut	94.85	10.09
Canard Duchêne Demi Sec	95.90	10.20
Charles de Cazenove Rosé	99.90	10.62
Mercier Brut	99.90	10.62
Hubert de Claminger Brut	99.90	10.62
Charles de Cazenove	99.90	10.62
Castellane	101.40	10.78
Vranken 1990	106.15	11.29
Lanson Black Label Brut	109.70	11.67
Mumm Cordon Rouge	115.30	12.26
Piper Heidsieck Brut	115.65	12.30
Laurent Perrier Brut	118.70	12.62
Perrier Jouet Grand Brut	119.90	12.75
Charles Heidsieck Brut Réserve	124.95	13.29
Moët et Chandon Brut	126.80	13.49
Pommery Brut	128.35	13.65
Canard Duchêne Rosé	128.80	13.70
Lanson Ivory Label Demi Sec	130.00	13.82
Veuve Clicquot Ponsardin Brut	134.85	14.34
Mumm Cordon Rosé Brut	139.50	14.84
Moët et Chandon Brut 1er Cru	144.00	15.31
Charles Lafitte Brut 1989	148.90	15.84
President Brut	154.90	16.47
Pommery 1991	161.00	17.12
Veuve Clicquot Ponsardin 1990	194.55	20.69

Beer	% Vol	FF	£
Alsabrau 10 x 25cl	4.5	11.00	1.17
Alsa Brun 24 x 25cl	4.5	27.95	2.97
Bière Blonde 24 x 25cl (Carrefour's own)	4.6	34.80	3.70
Artenbrau 24 x 50cl	5.0	37.30	3.96
St Omer Pils 24 x 25cl	5.0	37.95	4.03
Facon Blonde 24 x 25cl	4.9	39.90	4.24
33 Export 24 x 25cl	4.8	41.50	4.41
Kanterbrau 24 x 25cl	4.7	43.95	4.67
Semeuse 25 x 25cl	5.0	45.55	4.84
Stella Artois 24 x 25cl	5.2	49.50	5.26
Kronenbourg 26 x 25cl	4.7	52.00	5.53
St Omer 24 x 50cl	5.0	85.80	9.12
Becks 24 x 33cl	5.0	139.00	14.78
Caffreys 24 x 25cl	4.8	159.90	17.01

Continent Hypermarket

Ave Georges Guyneme,
Calais

Map Ref:	F4
Bus Nos:	2 & 4
English:	No
Tasting:	No
Payment:	£, 💳 💳
Parking:	Yes
Open:	Monday to Saturday 8.30am-9.30pm
Closed:	Sunday

How To Get There

Exit the port at Calais and turn left. Then follow the sign for A26 autoroute.

After around 5 minutes take exit at junction (sortie) 3. Continue until you see signs for Continent.

Continent hypermarket dominates a large shopping complex similar in style to Auchan.

As you would expect it has a huge range of products and carries many 'promos' (special offers). However, the shopping experience here is slightly dulled by the lack of brightness and the dingy decor.

There is reasonable range of mostly French wines including good Burgundies and Bordeaux wines.

There is usually a good selection of competitively priced champagnes alongside a range of beers

Continent also have a good range of spirits. See the Tipple Table for prices.

What's On Offer At Continent?
Quantities 75cl unless otherwise shown. Prices in-store are in French Francs (FF) converted to Sterling (£) here for your convenience at a rate FF9.40 to £1.00.

Sparkling Wine	FF	£
Muscat Roy Doux & Rosé Doux	10.50	1.11
Courcelles Blanc de Blancs Demi Sec	14.90	1.58
Opéra Blanc de Blanc Demi Sec & Brut	15.40	1.63
Asti	21.95	2.33
Charles Volner Demis Sec	23.83	2.53
Veuve Crezance Brut	23.90	2.54
Charles Volner Brut	23.80	2.53
Cordornice Brut	24.95	2.65
Vouvray	25.31	2.69
Café de Paris Blanc de Blanc Demi Sec	27.50	2.92
Blanquet de Limoux Brut & Demi Sec	28.90	3.07

Sparkling Wine contd		FF	£
Kriter Brut de Brut		28.95	3.07
Clairette de Die Brut		29.10	3.09
Saumur Ackerman		29.54	3.14
Aimery Demi Sec		29.95	3.18
Blanc Foussy		30.95	3.29
Veuve Amiot Brut & Demi Sec		31.50	3.35
Saumur Gratien & Meyer		34.95	3.71
Crémant de Bourgogne		37.95	4.03

Champagne		FF	£
Larmigny Brut		69.90	7.43
Keller Brut		74.90	7.96
De Castellane Brut		82.35	8.76
Henry Gonlet Brut		82.95	8.82
G H Martel & Co		83.50	8.88
Chanoine Brut		84.50	8.98
Vranken		84.95	9.03
Keller Rosé		87.90	9.35
Leonce D'Albe		89.95	9.56
Canard Duchêne Demi Sec & Brut		94.96	10.10
Mercier Brut Rosé		104.00	11.06
Piper Heidsieck		109.99	11.70
President Brut		110.00	11.70
Germain 1990 Brut		113.00	12.02
Mumm Cordon Rouge		119.95	12.76
Laurent Perrier Brut		120.51	12.68
Pommery Brut		124.64	13.25
Moët et Chandon Brut		126.81	13.49
Taittinger		135.00	14.36
Lanson Brut Rosé		139.95	14.88
Laurent Perrier Rosé Brut		176.07	18.73
Alfred Rothschild & Co Brut		199.50	21.22

Beers	% Vol	FF	£
Carlsberg 6 x 25cl	5.5	20.35	2.16
Kronenbourg Leger 10 x 25cl	2.6	21.45	2.28
Koenigsbier 24 x 25cl	2.6	26.90	2.86
Koenigsbier 24 x 25cl	3.7	27.95	2.97
Bruckbier Blonde 24 x 25cl	4.7	34.90	3.71
La Facon Blonde 24 x 25cl	4.9	39.95	4.25
St Omer Pils 24 x 25cl	5.0	41.25	4.38
Kanterbrau 24 x 25cl	4.7	41.64	4.42
33 Export 24 x 25cl	4.8	41.65	4.43
Kronenbourg 26 x 25cl	4.7	52.50	5.58
Stella Artois 24 x 25cl	5.2	119.95	12.66
Amsterdam Mariner 24 x 33cl	5.0	129.95	13.82
Fosters Lager 24 x 50cl	5.0	139.95	14.88
Caffreys 24 x 50cl	4.8	159.95	17.01

La Boutique Sainsbury's

Forty Nieulay, Route de Boulogne (RN1)
Tel: 00 33 3 21 968 150

Map Ref: A5
Bus No: 5 (take it from the railway station)
English: Yes
Tasting: Promotion wines only
Payments: £, VISA ⬤⬤
Parking: Yes
Open: Monday to Saturday 8.30am-9pm
Closed: Sunday

How To Get There

From the ferry terminal take the motorway following the signs for Boulogne and exit at junction (sortie) 12 or 14 following signs to Coquelles.
From Le Shuttle take the A16 motorway following signs for Calais exit (sortie) 14 then follow signs for Auchan Sainsburys

BEST VALUE CROSS CHANNEL CHAMPAGNE
Sainsburys Extra Dry Champagne
FF95/£9.69

BEST CROSS CHANNEL ROSE
1995 Mount Hurtle Grenache Rosé
FF30/£3.19

SPECIAL OFFER: Spend over £20 and get a **Free** bottle of the Paul Mason Carafe

Although Sainsbury's does not have the largest selection of wines in Calais, probably due to lack of space, they do have a variety of consistently good wines from around the globe. This year their Extra Dry Champagne has won our Best Value Cross-Channel Champagne award.

The off-licence style outlet contains a world-wide selection of affordable wines especially from the New World. For instance the 1995 Mount Hurtle Grenache Rosé from Oz has won our Best Cross-Channel Rosé award.

The spirits tend to be Sainsbury's own and beers will not be featuring on their shelves this year. *'We are keen to use the available space for even more great wines'* explained Nico Thiriot, Sainsbury's Product Manager.

⭐ STAR BUYS ⭐
Sainsbury's Extra Dry Champagne FF95/£10.06
The label describes the contents as delicate and elegant. This accurately describes its gentle and flowery attributes.

1997 Beaujolais Les Roches Grillés FF21/£2.23
Pungent, smooth fruit with real depth and a lively, peppery finish.

1995 Mount Hurtle Grenache Rosé FF30/£3.19
Another award winning wine from Sainsbury. A dark, rich, tangy, heady Australian Rosé.

1997 Fleurie La Madone FF44/£4.66
A wine with steady structure, from a good vintage. Smooth and peppery on the palate.

1994 La Vielle Cure, Fronsac FF50/£5.30
Dark colour, earthy scents, good depth and tangy oak. Serious and chewy.

1995 Fairview Cabernet Sauvignon
Pungent fruit, warm, ripe, curranty with a detectable zing of green fruit.

Franck Galand, Sainsbury's friendly manager is shown here dealing with an enquiry

Tesco Vin Plus

Cité Europe
Coquelles

Map Ref: A6
Bus No: 7
English: Yes
Tasting: Sporadically
Payment: £, VISA ●●
Parking: Yes
Open: Monday-Saturday
            9am-10pm
Closed: Sunday

How To Get There

From the port turn left and continue onto the A26 motorway. Follow signs to Dunkerque onto the A16 motorway. Exit at Junction (sortie) 18 and follow signs to Boulogne. Exit at Junction (sortie) 12. Then follow signs to Cité de la Europe, Centre Commercial until you get to Cité Europe. Tesco is on the lower level.

In true supermarket style Tesco is brightly lit and well laid out. They complement this with the very British 'car service' whereby you can obtain your purchases later from the collection point. This is definitely a blessing and a good alternative to carrying your shopping with you while you tour the rest of Cité Europe.

You will find a huge range of 1000 wines in all price ranges and quality alongside many regional products. There is also a vast selection of beers and spirits.

★ STAR BUYS ★

1992 Merlot Haskovo Reserve FF21.70/£2.30
Dark and well-wooded fruit, good depth, in black pastille style, sweet and well-aged.

1996 Temple Breuer Cornucopia Grenache FF46.50/£4.94
Lots of stewy rich Australian flavour - sweet, rich and somewhat tangy.

1987 Raimat Cabernet Sauvignon FF60.00/£6.38

Lashings of soft oak and simmered, soupy yet classy aged fruit. Rich, subtle and long.

1995 Errazuriz Cabernet Sauvignon Reserva FF59.90/£6.37

Lots of blackcurrant and bramble fruit, lush with soft black fruit. It has intensity and is well-balanced.

Reka Valley Hungarian Chardonnay FF13.90/£1.47

A pleasantly perfumed wine in a muscat way. Juicy to taste. Good value at less than £1.50 a bottle.

Cabernet de Saumur Rosé FF21.90/£2.32

Not much on the nose but light plum fruit on the palate. A decent full-fruited guzzle, off dry and clean.

Rosé d'Anjou FF13.90/£1.47

Very sweet and quaffable, probably one of the better Rosé d'Anjous available in Calais.

1997 McLaren Vale Chardonnay, Maglieri FF40.90/£4.35

Rich in oak on the nose and this follows through to the palate. A classic syrupy Oz style. Not everyone's cup of tea but go for it if you like an 'in your face' flavour.

1997 Jackson Estate Sauvignon Blanc FF58.99/£6.27/£6.27

Vinous and quite French in style, clean and taut.

1997 Chapel Hill Unwooded Chardonnay FF58.99/£6.27

Succulent Ausie fruit and decent lush Chardonnay.

1996 Tim Adams Semillon FF59.90/£6.37

Another Aussie classic, but semillon this time, good and tangy.

1996 Chablis, Cuvée Claude Dominique FF45.00/£4.78

Intense, vivid with fresh green citrus and firm apple flavours.

Chilean Chardonnay FF20.00/£2.12
Though an unsubtle wine, who cares, it offers lots of zing and tang instead.

1990 Vintage Champagne FF150.00/£15.95
If you like pear drops, go for it.

Tesco Cava FF23.90/£2.54
A touch of sweetness, a little flowery but crisp and clean too.

Premier Cru Champagne FF85.90/£9.13
Nice, yeasty stuff with a ripe edge to it. Classic and worth buying at this price

What's On Offer At Tesco?
Quantities 75cl unless otherwise shown. Prices in-store are in French Francs (FF) converted to Sterling (£) here for your convenience at a rate FF9.4 to £1.00. The third column is the price in Tesco in the UK.

Sparkling wine	FF	£	UK £
Tesco Moscato Spumante	8.70	0.92	3.09
Pol Remy Demi Sec	8.90	0.94	-
Pol Remy Brut	9.90	1.04	-
Tesco Asti Spumante	22.50	2.38	4.99
Tesco Cava & Rosé Sparkling Wine	23.90	2.53	4.99
Tesco South. African Sauvignon Blanc	25.90	2.74	4.99
Tesco Australian Sparkling Wine	25.90	2.74	4.99
Kriter Demi Sec	29.00	3.07	-
Alsace Cremant Blanc de Blancs	29.90	3.17	-
Tesco Blanquette de Limoux	30.90	3.27	6.99
Martini Asti Spumante	31.00	3.28	5.49
Kriter Brut & Rosé	32.00	3.39	-
Tesco Vintage Cava	33.50	3.55	6.99
Martini Brut Sparkling	33.50	3.55	6.49
Angus Brut & Brut Rosé	33.90	3.59	6.49
Sparkling Saumur	39.00	4.13	5.99
Lindauer Rosé	40.90	4.33	7.49
Tesco Crémant de Bourgogne	40.90	4.33	6.99
Freixenet Cordon Negro Brut	42.90	4.54	7.49
Lindauer New Zealand Sparkling Wine	44.90	4.76	7.49
Yalumba Cabernet Sauvignon	55.90	5.92	8.49
Mumm Cuvée Napa	60.90	6.45	9.99

Tesco Supermarket

Champagne	FF	£	UK £
Champagne St Maurice	59.90	6.35	-
Paul Letrier Champagne	65.00	6.89	9.99
Canard Duchêne Brut	85.40	9.05	-
Tesco Champagne Brut	85.90	9.10	-
Nicolas Feuillate Brut & Demi Sec & Rose	89.00	9.43	-
Tesco Blanc de Noirs Champagne	90.90	9.63	9.99
Canard Duchêne Demi Sec	95.90	10.16	-
Tesco Blanc de Blancs	100.00	10.60	13.99
Mercier Brut Champagne	105.00	11.13	16.99
Piper Heidsieck Demi-Sec	110.00	11.66	17.99
Mercier Demi-Sec	115.00	12.19	16.99
Piper Heidsieck Brut NV	130.00	13.78	17.99
Lanson Black Label	135.00	14.31	18.99
Moët & Chandon Brut Imperial	135.00	14.31	19.99
Nicolas Feuillate Vintage	148.00	15.69	-
Charles Lafitte Champagne 1985	149.00	15.80	17.99
Louis Roederer Brut Premier	149.00	15.80	23.99
Tesco Vintage Champagne	150.00	15.90	19.79
Veuve Clicquot Brut NV	150.00	15.90	22.99
Charles Heidsieck Champagne	165.00	17.49	21.99
Taittinger Brut Reserve	190.00	20.14	22.99
Bollinger	200.00	21.20	25.99
Moët & Chandon Vintage Champagne	200.00	21.20	26.99
Palme D'Or Nicolas Feuillate	349.00	37.00	-
Bollinger Vintage Champagne	315.00	33.40	41.99
Dom Perignon Vintage Champagne	430.00	45.59	59.99

Beer	% Vol	FF	£	UK £
Bière D'Alsace Lager 10 x 25cl	n/a	13.90	1.47	3.99
Vin Plus Bière de Lux 24 x 25cl	n/a	29.95	3.17	4.99
St Omer 24 x 25cl	5.0%	34.30	3.63	-
Tesco Best Bitter 12 x 44cl	n/a	25.00	3.71	6.29
Stella Artois 24 x 25cl	5.0%	52.95	5.61	10.95
Becks Bier 12 x 27.5cl bottles	5.0%	59.00	6.25	10.99
Kronenbourg 26 x 25cl	5.0%	64.00	6.78	-
Heineken Lager 24 x 44cl cans	3.4%	70.00	7.42	15.99
Bishops Finger Strong Ale 12 x 50cl	5.4%	99.00	10.49	-
Carling Black Label	4.1%	99.00	10.49	15.99
John Smiths Bitter 24 x 44cl	n/a	114.50	12.14	19.79
Boddingtons Draught Bitter 24 x 50cl	3.8%	139.00	14.74	17.99

Beer Lovers

Rue de Verdun 62100
Calais
Tel: 00 33 321 97 72 00

Map Ref: B4
Bus No: 4
English: Yes
Tasting: Not much
Payment: £, VISA mastercard
Parking: Yes
Open: 24 hours
           Monday -Friday
           From 10pm-6am
           Saturday & Sunday

How To Get There

From the port take the St Omer Paris motorway for 2.3 miles, then turn off the Boulogne motorway (towards Boulogne) for 2/3 miles until exit (sortie) 14. Turn right here and straight over the roundabout for 300 yards.

Beer Lovers is on the left.

Beer Lovers is a warehouse style cash and carry with many cheap and cheerful wines alongside some finer contemporary wines.

They are also a good source of beer and their own label Beer Lovers Beer is a bargain at £3.25 for 24 bottles.

SPECIAL OFFER

Spend FF300 and get a **Free** bottle of Santiago Chilean wine.
Choose from red, white or rosé

 STAR BUYS

1997 Chablis premier Cru, Henry de Villamont £6.72

An incisive, ripe and intense example. Some honeysuckle notes here.

1996 Muscadet Sèvre et Maine, La Butte du Moulin, £2.33

You can taste a little bready yeast beneath its piercing and incisive quality. Quite mouthwatering.

1997 Cuvée Clemence, Entre-Deux-Mers £2.72
A well-expressed, complex and integrated wine. Great oakey nose too suported by fruit in the background. A very good buy at this price and probably the best Entre-Deux-Mers in Calais.

1995 Château Les Jonquerelles £2.72
Nice fresh scents. This wine has a rather biting, bitter, mineral edge to it.

1996 Château Tuileries-Gourribon, Côtes du Bourg £3.88
Light, dry, sound claret.

What's On Offer at Beer Lovers
Wine Quantities 75cl unless otherwise indicated.
Prices instore are in Sterling.

Sparkling wine	% Vol	£
Duc de Marchipont Demi Sec & Brut		0.75
Paul Bur Blanc de Blancs		1.89
Pol Remy Magnum		2.74
Francois d'Orbay Blanc de Blancs		3.14
Cuvée Jean Jacques Blanc de Blancs		3.26
Champagne		£
Paul Robert		7.48
Veuve Renard		7.50
Venoge Brut		11.50
Moët et Chandon		13.90
Beer	**% Vol**	**£**
Belzebuth 24 x 25cl (plus free glass)	5.0	2.72
Beer Lovers Beer 24 x 25cl	5.1	3.25
Marten's 24 x 25cl	5.0	3.36
Amsterdam Mariner 24 x 33cl	5.0	4.55
Stella Artois 24 x 25cl	5.2	5.05
Alsatia 24 x 25cl	5.1	5.15
33 Export 24 x 25cl	4.8	5.15
Grölsch 24 x 25cl	5.0	5.68
Robert Cains 24 x 50cl	4.0	9.25
Amsterdam Mariner 24 x 50cl	5.0	9.26

Beer Lovers Cash & Carry

Beer contd.	% Vol	£
Skona 24 x 50cl	8.6	10.10
Crest Super 24 x 50cl	10.0	11.67
Tangle Foot 24 x 50cl	5.0	12.09
Dempseys 24 x 50cl	4.8	12.10
Grölsch 24 x 50cl	5.0	13.15
Becks 24 x 33cl	5.0	13.27
Carling Black Label 24 x 50cl	4.1	13.28
Caffreys 24 x 44cl	4.8	13.37
Fosters 24 x 50cl	5.0	13.48
Bishop's Finger 24 x 44cl	5.4	13.55
Budweiser Budvar 24 x 33cl	5.0	14.24
John Smiths Bitter 24 x 44cl	4.0	15.46
Fosters Ice 24 x 33cl	5.0	16.16
Draught Guinness 24 x 44cl	4.1	19.25

Beer Lovers' outlet

Boozers

RN43
Route de Saint Omer
62100 Calais
Tel: 00 33 321 19 17 17

Map Ref: G7
Bus No: -
English: Yes
Tasting: Yes
Payment: £, VISA ⬤⬤
Parking: Yes
Open: 7.00am - 9.30pm
            daily

How To Get There

From the port turn left and take the A26 motorway and onto A16 intersection (direction of Boulogne) and take first exit (sortie 17) for St. Omer.

From Boulogne take A16 motorway (direction of Calais/Dunkirk). Take exit (sortie 17) to St Omer

Special Offer

Enjoy a **5%** discount on all wines on presentation of your Channel Hopper's Guide

Boozers almost salutes you as you drive along the A16 motorway. You simply cannot miss it, with its huge neon sign and zepplin floating above it. It even comes complete with its own slogan 'the spirit of Calais'. With a name like Boozers, and a gimmick for a slogan it conjures up images of beer swilling staff selling to beer swilling bootleggers from a dusty tacky warehouse.

I could not have been more wrong. The interior is well-groomed, nicely decorated with a friendly atmosphere. There is a small cafe style section where you can sit a while and enjoy a cup of coffee.

Boozers was established in February 1998 and so it is still a newcomer to the area. Naturally, Boozers is keen to make its mark on the cross-Channel trade. Ray Culver the manager, says his aim is to create a a convivial environment:

Boozers

'Customers can taste wines at the wine bar' Ray says with a grin 'and then I give them a bit of gyp, they give me a bit of gyp and we all have a laugh'. That's the spirit! - of Calais?

 ★ STAR BUYS ★

1997 Merlot, Louis Eschenauer, Vin de Pays d'Oc £1.70
An easy drinking, soft gentle, smooth wine.

1996 Sancerre Rosé, Le Bastard de Paracy £5.85
A lovely salmon pink hue is complemented with gentle fruit scents. It is very dry with tart cherry and strawberry fruit.

Cuvée de la Chevalière Cabernet Perlant Demi Sec £4.10
Soft, full sweet edged flavours. A good fun wine.

Frog's Piss, £1.99 !?
The sign says 'don't ask', so I didn't!

What's On Offer At Boozers?
Quantities 75cl unless otherwise shown. Prices in-store are shown in Sterling (£).

Sparkling wine	£
Baron de Rothberg Brut & Demi Sec	1.00
Chamsource Blanc de Blancs Brut	1.75
Asti Moscato	2.50
Vincent Edouard Poiner	2.70
Saumur Rosé	3.50
Asti	3.55
Louis de Grenelle Saumur	4.05
Cuvée de la Chevalierie Cabernet Perland Demi Sec Red	4.10
Saumur Demi-Sec	4.10
Crémant de Loire Demi-Sec & Rosé	4.25
Crémant de Loire Louis de Grenelle	4.50
Champagne	£
B Martin	7.65
A Bergère	8.80
Autréau Roualet Brut	9.50
Cl. de la Chapelle	10.90
Brut Blanc de Noirs de Venoge	15.00
Pommery Brut Rosé	22.50

Beer	% Vol	£
Masbräu 24 x 25cl	4.5	2.99
Amos 24 x 25cl	4.8	3.30
St Omer 24 x 25cl	5.0	4.40
Amsterdam Mariner 24 x 33cl	5.0	4.95
Stella Artois 24 x 25cl	5.2	5.30
Grölsch 24 x 25cl cans	5.0	5.85
Chinese Ginseng Beer 24 x 33cl	5.6	7.00
Amsterdam Mariner 24 x 50cl	5.0	9.30
Stella Artois 24 x 50cl	5.2	11.25
Foster's Lager 24 x 50cl	5.0	11.50
Kronenbourg 64 24 x 44cl	5.0	11.75
Grölsch 24 x 50cl	5.0	11.75
Newcastle Brown Ale 24 x 33cl	4.5	12.30
Becks 24 x 33cl	5.0	12.50
McEwans 24 x 50cl	4.1	12.75
Dempsey 24 x 50cl	4.8	13.10
Tangle Foot 24 x 50cl	5.0	13.20
Carlsberg 24 x 44cl	4.2	14.25
Caffrey's 24 x 44cl	4.8	14.30
Red Strip 24 x 50cl	4.7	14.50
Guinness Original 24 x 44cl	4.3	14.50
Labbatts Ice 24 x 33cl	5.6	14.50
Skol Super 24 x 50cl	9.2	14.60
Kestrel Lager 24 x 50cl	9.0	14.70
John Smith 24 x 50cl	4.0	15.00
Newcastle Brown Ale 24 x 50cl	4.7	15.00
Budweiser 24 x 33cl	5.0	15.50
Foster's Ice 24 x 33cl	5.0	15.50
Beamish Irish Stout 24 x 44cl	4.2	15.75
Tennent's Super 24 x 50cl	9.0	15.95
Guinness Draught 24 x 44cl	4.2	16.95
Holsten 24 x 33cl	5.5	17.50
Carlsberg Special Brew 24 x 44cl	9.0	17.80

Le Chai Ardrésien Cash & Carry

Le Chai Ardrésien

Route Nationale
Bois en Ardres 62610
Ardres
Tel: 00 33 321 36 2626

Map Ref: Follow the road at G8
Bus No: -
English: Yes.
Tasting: Yes, it is encouraged
Payment: £, [visa] [mastercard]
Parking: In front, side & rear
Open: 10am-6pm
            6 days a week
Closed: Sunday

How To Get There

From the Calais turn left onto the motorway, take the second exit and the immediate next exit onto RN43 (i.e Route de St Omer). On arriving at Ardres, midway to St Omer, Le Chais Ardrésien is on the left just past the first roundabout. From Boulogne, take the A16, come off at junction (sortie) 17 then follow the RN43 as per Calais.

Not strictly in Calais, but if you make the 15 minute detour you will be rewarded with a range of over 1400 wines representing all the areas of France.

The husband and wife team of Paul and Bea Jones made their dream come true by establishing Le Chai Ardrésien in May 1993. The outlet comes complete with a 'dégustation' table where tasting on a generous selection of wines is always available.

For a serious tasting though, Paul and Bea welcome parties of 4 to 100 people to enjoy their Le Chai Wine Experience. For £15.00 per head, they lay on a lavish buffet and unlimited wine tasting. You also get to taste port, whisky, brandies and liqueurs. Salut! to an enjoyable and heady experience.

Le Chai Ardrésien have expanded their Kosher wines again (over 200 now including Champagne). Those with Barmitzvahs or weddings coming up may be interested to know that personalised labels can be arranged. To complement this they also sell frozen kosher meat and veal.

The Jones' run a Members Wine Club. This entitles you to a 15% discount on all their products and invitations to wine tastings with buffets. Members also become eligible to join a unique system of investing in and receiving bonus wines. Ask instore for details.

To Join the club simply pop in with a passport photo or send it to them by post. Club membership fee is £25 annually.

The large and spacious Le Chai Adrésien with wines from all regions of France.

Le Chais Wine Merchant

Le Chais

40 rue de Phalsbourg,
62100 Calais
Tel: 00 33 321978857

Map Ref: E3
Bus No: 2
English: A little
Tasting: Some
Payment: £,   💳 💳
Parking: Yes
Open: 9am-7pm daily
Closed: 12pm-2pm daily

How To Get There

On exiting the port turn right following the sign to Centre Ville. At the roundabout take the second exit.
At the end of the road turn right into rue Mollien. At the traffic lights turn right. Continue for 100 yards. Le Chais is on the right.

SPECIAL OFFER:

Receive a 5% discount on all your wine purchases (This offer does not include promotion wines)

To be eligible, you must remember to show your Channel Hopper's Guide.

Le Chais is one of many dotted around France. There is an outlet in Boulogne and a small outlet in Cité Europe. Le Vins France are also part of the group. Founded in 1865 Le Chais is the oldest wine merchant in the area.

Le Chais Wine Merchant

They specialise in French wine mainly from Bordeaux from years 1966 to 1996. Names on the shelves include Jadot and Guigal

 ⭐ STAR BUYS ⭐

1997 Les Vigneaux, Vin de pays d'Oc Cabernet Sauvignon £1.25
A very good value meaty edged wine, full of ripe fruits, soft with a gutsy style. Lashings of flavour.

1997 Beaujolais Rosé, Gabriel Remuet £1.98
This Beaujolais has an attractive scent of currants. It is clean and fresh on the palate with piercing redcurrant fruit. Chill first.

1996 Crozes-Hermitage, Les Meysonniers, Chapoutier £6.68
Appealing yet incisive perfumed Syrah nose. Almost taste the perfume in the flavour. Intense, long with deeply plum flavours.

1997 Gaillac White, Château Lecusse £2.50
A typical Southern French white wine, full, soft and vegetal in flavour

1996 Gaillac Red, Château Lecusse £2.50
A very dark Gaillac with smoky aromas, full, vivid and fairly rounded. Lots of flavour though a tad spikey.

1996 Pinot Noir Vieilles Vignes, Vins de Pays du Franche Comté, Vignoble Guillaume £3.30
Another great value wine. A great Burgundy style Pinot Noir, perfumed and elegant. Best lightly chilled.

1995 Château Les Tuileries de Déroc, Graves de Vayres £3.90
A softly earthy claret lots of minerals and earth behind soft, gentle plum exterior. Typical in style.

1995 Château Roudier, Montagne St Emilion £4.90
If you like meaty, earthy rustic, tannic style wines, this is for you. It gives off scents of warm, raw liver, filled with earthy tannic extract. A gutsy mouthful.

Le Chais Wine Merchant

What's On Offer At Le Chais?
Quantities 75cl unless otherwise shown. Prices in-store are in French Francs (FF) converted to Sterling (£) here for your convenience at a rate FF9.40 to £1.00.

Sparkling Wine		FF	£
Mousseux Brut & Demi Sec		8.90	.94
Cava Saint Clair Brut		23.80	2.53
Chardonnay Blanc de Blancs		25.00	2.65
Rosé de Saignee		25.00	2.65
Brummel Blanc de Blancs		25.80	2.74
Asti		26.80	2.85
Chardonnay Cherakerde		28.00	2.97
Crémant de Loire		29.80	3.17
Bouvet Ladubay Saumur Brut		39.80	4.23
Bouvet Ladubay Millesime		45.00	4.78
Bouvet Rubis Excellence (Red) Sweet		45.00	4.78

Champagne		FF	£
Maurice Leger Epernay		69.80	7.42
Bredon Reims		72.80	7.74
Monbelian 1er Cru Venteuil		72.80	7.74
J P Marniquet 1er Cru Venteuil		79.80	8.48
Vueve Le Pitre 1er Cru Rully		89.80	9.55
Jacquart Mosaique		99.80	10.61
Lanson Black Label		105.00	11.23
Piper Heidsieck		112.00	11.91
Pol Roger		114.00	12.12
Moët et Chandon		135.00	14.36
Veuve Clicquot		138.00	14.68
Louis Roederer		139.80	14.87
Lanson Millesime 1990 and Rosé		155.00	16.48
Bollinger		159.80	17.00
Laurent Perrier Rosé		178.00	18.93

Beers	% Vol	FF	£
Upsteim 24 x 25cl	5.2	34.00	3.61
Nordheim 24 x 25cl	4.7	35.00	3.72
Stella Artois Collectivite 24 x 25cl	5.2	49.00	5.21
33 Export 24 x 25cl	4.8	49.50	5.26
Amsterdam Mariner 24 x 25cl	5.0	55.00	5.85
1664 24 x 33cl	6.3	95.00	10.10
Grölsch 25 x 50cl	5.0	110.00	11.70
Becks 24 x 33cl	4.7	115.00	12.23
Tangle Foot 24 x 50cl	5.0	119.00	12.65
Dempsey's 24 x 50cl	4.8	119.50	12.71
Carling Black Label 24 x 50cl	5.0	125.00	13.29
Budweiser Budvar 24 x 33cl	5.0	136.00	14.46
John Smith Ex.Smooth 24 x 44cl	4.0	148.00	15.74
Caffrey's 24 x 44cl	4.8	158.00	16.80

Eastenders

14 rue Gustav Courbet,
Zone Marcel Doret
Tel: 00 33 321 34 53 33

Map Ref: H4
Bus No: -
English: Yes
Tasting: No
Payment: £,
Parking: Yes
Open: 24 hours daily

BEST CROSS CHANNEL DRINKS WAREHOUSE

BEST CROSS-CHANNEL RED WINE
1996 Château Tour des Gendres, Bergerac, £2.60

JOINT BEST VALUE CROSS-CHANNEL RED WINE
1995 Guigal Côtes du Rhône, £3.50

RUNNER UP BEST VALUE CROSS-CHANNEL CHAMPAGNE
Champagne Millenium, £9.95

How To Get There

From the Calais ferry terminal turn left onto the A26 motorway and come off at the first junction you come to, junction (sortie) 3 following the sign to Z A Marcel Doret and continue to the roundabout where you will be able to see Eastenders.

From Boulogne follow directions to the A16 motorway to Calais. Come off at Junction 18 (sign posted Ports) and exit at junction (sortie) 3 following the sign to Z A Marcel Doret.

ABSOLUTELY FREE!!

A bottle of Eastender's own Lovely Bubbley sparkling wine only on presentation of this guide

Only one per customer

Eastenders Cash & Carry

Eastenders is run by one man and his dog - and Dave West is some man. From Romford barrow boy to bootleggers' dream in a mere decade, steadily building Eastenders into an empire in Calais. And the dog! Less said the better!

This outlet is one of three in Calais and is the best of the three. It's literally a large warehouse - no frills here - just lots of wines, lots of beer, lots of dust, chaotic but full of surprises. We found many good wines to recommend and these follow below.

However, one wine which must have amused Dave West to submit into the wine tasting - the Dog's Bollocks - was good for a laugh. At £1.00 it is worth buying to create an effect at your next dinner party! Serve it, though, at your peril and only if you are prepared never to see your dinner guests again.

If you like soft drinks you can buy coke and pepsi max here for £5 and £4.50 a case of 24 respectively. That's 21p and 18p a can!

The spirit selection is small but seems well-priced. For instance 1 litre of Traitor's Gate vodka costs £7.00.

Amongst some own-label products such as Eastenders Lovely Bubbly at just £1.00 is Eastenders' own brand of beer: ESP. This great tasting beer is available in two strengths 5.2% and 9.2% both of which are great value at 17p and 23p respectively per 25cl bottle! What does ESP stand for? 'Extra Sex Please' said Dave West with a cheeky grin.

 STAR BUYS

Don Marino III, Rioja Crianza £2.25
Don't be put off by the label. This soft, rich,full and appealing wine represents great value.

1996 Château Tour des Gendres, Bergerac, £2.60
Good depth of colour. A deliciously lush wine, full of curranty fruit, with zing and tannins and with a mineral backdrop. Super value.

1995 Guigal Côtes du Rhône, £3.50.

What a bargain! A well-made classic red wine from the Rhône. Ripe, lush smooth-textured yet with dark spice in the flavour. Its rich in texture and just glides over your tastebuds on its way down.

1992 Sterling Hills, South Australia Cabernet Sauvignon, £3.50

A good value wine from down under. It's very dark, wheaty and stewed on the palate. It also has an impressive sediment.

1993 Cesari Amarone della Valpolicella £6.95

You get a hefty alcoholic content of 14% for the price. Sweet raisins in the background, and intensely fruited, deep and long. A dried-fruit symphony.

Sparkling Chardonnay, £2.25 (or £2 per bottle if bought by the case)

Straightforward, sweet and simple. Although quaffable on its own, you can dress it up with cassis to create a Kir Royal or with orange juice to make a Bucks Fizz.

Great Western Brut Rosé, £2.80

Uncomplicated pink fizz, with lots of soft vaguely peachy fruit. Ideal to add a little sparkle to any party.

Puilly-Fumé, Domaine Chatelain, Jean-Claude Chatelain, £4.95

Typical of its style, lots of nettle zing to it.

Chablis Premier Cru Fourchaume, Domaine de l'Englantière, Durup, £6.95

A classic premier Cru Chablis. Green fruit and quite sour. Lay it down for a year or two.

Millennium Cuvée Spéciale, £9.95

A well-made Champagne, with fabulous depth of flavour, with fruit biscuit elements. Delicious !

Louis Bourdiol Merlot, Vin de Pays D'Oc, £1.40

It emits a rather pleasant baked, stewed fruit aroma. Although a little thin, it has enough depth at the price.

1995 Crianza Navarra, Gran Fuedo, Julian Chivite £2.75

Lots of fruit in this Spanish red. An interesting mix of damson and fig - a gutsy mouthful.

Eastenders Cash & Carry

What's On Offer At Eastenders?
Quantities 75cl unless otherwise shown. Prices in-store are in Sterling (£)

Sparkling wine	FF	£
Lambrusco Bianco & Rosé & Red, Donelli	-	1.00
Spumante, Burti Italian	-	1.00
Römer, German	-	1.00
Roy de France Brut & Demi Sec	-	1.00
Garcia Real Sangria	-	1.25
Deinhard Yello, German	-	1.50
Paul de Coste Brut & Demi-Sec	-	1.75
André Californian sparkling wine	-	1.95
La Cotte Sauvignon Brut, S. African	-	2.00
Capetta Asti Italian	-	2.25
Seppelt Great Western Brut S. E. Australia	-	2.60
Yalada Reserve Brut & Rosé Australian	-	2.75
Château Reynella Brut, Australian	-	2.83
Faustino Cava Demi Sec	-	3.08
YalumbaAngus Brut & Rosé Australian	-	3.33
Blossom Hill Californian sparkling wine	-	3.75
Faustino Cava Brut, Spanish	-	3.75
Crémant D'Alsace	-	3.75
Killawara Brut & Rosé, S.E Australia	-	3.75
E&J Indigo Hills Chardonnay, Californian	-	3.95
Seaview Brut, S.E. Australia	-	3.95
Freixenet Cordon Negro, Spanish	-	4.00
Seppelt Pinot/Chardonnay 1990 S.E. Australia	-	4.50
Cuvée One, Australian Pinot/Chardonnay	-	5.67
Seaview Pinot/Chardonnay 1994 S.E Australia	-	6.00
Seppelt Shiraz S.E. Australia Red	-	6.25

Champagne	FF	£
Raymond Henriot Brut	-	6.95
Millennium	-	9.95
de Nauroy Brut	-	12.50
Pol Roger	-	12.95
de Nauroy Rosé	-	13.50
Veuve Cliquot	-	13.55
Moët et Chandon	-	14.50
Veuve Cliquot 1990	-	16.50
Veuve Cliquot Rosé 1990	-	17.50

Beer	% Vol	FF	£
Uberland 24 x 25cl	4.5	-	3.50
Classic 24 x 25cl	5.0	-	3.75
ESP 24 x 25cl	5.2	-	4.00
Stella Artois 24 x 25cl	5.2	-	4.80
ESP 24 x 25cl	9.2	-	5.50
ESP 24 x 50cl	5.2	-	7.50
Holsten Pils 24 x 33cl	5.5	-	14.00
Carling Black Label 24 x 50cl	4.1	-	10.50
ESP 24 x 50cl	9.2	-	11.00
Stella Artois cans 24 x 50cl	5.2	-	11.50
Fosters 24 x 50cl	4.0	-	11.50
Grölsch 24 x 50cl	5.0	-	11.50
Budweiser Budvar 24 x 33cl	5.0	-	12.00
Kestrel Super Strength 24 x 50cl	9.0	-	13.00
Skol Super Strength 24 x 50cl	9.2	-	13.00
Strongbow Super 24 x 50cl	8.4	-	13.50
Guinness Original 24 x 50cl	4.3	-	14.00
Caffrey's 25 x 50cl	4.8	-	15.00
Tennents Super 24 x 50cl	9.0	-	15.00
Guinness Draught 24 x 50cl	4.1	-	17.00

The infamous Dave West outside his warehouse

Franglais Beer & Wine
CD 215, 62185
Frethun
Tel: 00 33 321 85 29 39

Map Ref:	A5
Bus No:	-
English:	Yes
Tasting:	Yes, extensive
Payment:	£, VISA mastercard
Parking:	Yes
Open:	Daily 9am-7.00 pm, Saturday 9am-6.30 pm
Closed:	Sunday 9.30am-6.00pm

THE BEST CROSS-CHANNEL WINE TASTING FACILITY

Franglais' wine tasting facility is second to none and the best I have seen in Calais or Boulogne. Olivier, the young, dynamic manager of Franglais explained why he invested so much in the state-of-the-art 'Bar A Vin' (wine bar) dispenser: 'All the wines on display on the in the 'Bar A Vin' are stored individually at its optimum temperature', he enthused,

How To Get There
From Calais:
On exiting the port turn left onto A16-A26 motorway towards Paris-Reims. Continue to the autoroute to the A16 intersection. Take the A16 signposted Boulogne. Continue to exit (sortie) 11 signposted Gare TGV. Leave the autoroute and turn left over the bridge (D215). Franglais is 900 yards ahead on the right.

From Boulogne:
Take the A16 motorway towards Calais and then as above.

SPECIAL OFFER:

Spend £25.00 or more and choose either a Chardonnay Taillan or a Cabernet Sauvignon Taillon Vin de Pays d'Oc.

You must present your Channel Hopper's Guide to be eligible.

'which means you get to taste the wine at its best. Some outlets offer a wine tasting service but the wines get left open all day and the customer gets a mouthful of vinegar. This could never happen with the Bar A Vin.'

Olivier is very keen to ensure customers get every opportunity to buy wines they like and the staff are happy to impart expert advice. Olivier in particular, does so with gusto.

The 300 strong wines range from the humble at 69p to Grand Crû Classé wines from Bordeaux and wines to lay down.

Unfortunately, we have not been able to taste many of Franglais wines in time for publication but here are at least two wines worth buying.

 ⭐ STAR BUYS ⭐

1996 Vin de Pays d'Oc Taillan Cabernet Sauvignon, £1.43
A gutsy wine at the price with some depth.

1996 Bordeaux Superieur, Chateau Cadouin-Segur, £2.55
This benefits from currant and liquorice scents and is earthy and grippy on the palate with a mineral finish. Decent value for money.

Olivier is seen here behind the state-of-the-art Bar A Vins

Franglais Beer & Wine

Sparkling wines		FF	£
Doriant Brut or Demi-Sec		7.95	.84
Baron de Rothberg Brut or Demi- Sec		8.95	.95
Spumante Orsola		11.65	1.23
Moscato Spumante		11.90	1.26
Charles Nimot Brut & Demi Sec		15.95	1.69
Chardonnay Blanc de Blanc Brut		19.95	2.12
Charles Roux Methode Traditionelle Brut & Demi Sec		19.95	2.12
Veuve Deville Rosé Brut		19.95	2.12
Marquis de Loire Methode Traditionelle Touraine		23.55	2.50
Asti Perlino		28.45	3.02
Vouvray Brut & Demi Sec		29.95	3.18
Crémant de Bordeaux Ruby Brut		34.95	3.71
Crémant Bourgogne 1994 Tasterinage Brut		42.00	4.46

Beers	Vol %	FF	£
Maltson Pils 24 x 25cl bottles	n/a	33.95	3.61
Bière de St Omer 24 x 25 bottles	5.0	34.90	3.71
Upsthem Biere Flanders 24 x 25cl	5.2	36.15	3.84
33 Export 24 x 25 cl bottles	4.8	46.65	4.96
Stella Artois 24 x 25 cl bottles	5.2	48.95	5.20
Bière de St Omer 25 x 50	5.0	79.90	8.50
Amsterdam Mariner 24 x 50cl	5.0	85.30	8.55
Dempsey 24 x 44cl	4.8	97.80	10.40
Badger Brewery 24 x 50cl	4.0	105.75	11.25
Bombardier 24 x 50cl	4.3	105.75	11.25
Stella Artois 24 x 50cl	5.2	109.50	10.89
Grölsch Dark Beer 24 x 50cl	5.0	119.35	11.18
Bavaria Strong 24 x 44cl	8.6	109.75	11.64
Rolling Rock 24 x 33cl bottles	5.0	111.65	11.87
Labatt Ice 24 x 33 bottles	5.6	116.75	12.42
Tangle Foot 24 x 50cl	5.2	117.35	12.48
Tetley's Bitter 24 x 25cl	n/a	117.75	12.52
Becks 24 x 33cl bottles	4.7	119.95	12.76
Crest Super 24 x 50 cl	10.0	123.55	13.14
Carling Black Label 24 x 50cl	4.1	126.10	13.41
Bishop's Finger 24 x 44cl	5.4	128.40	13.65
Budweiser 24 x 33cl	5.0	137.90	14.67
Carlsberg Lager 24 x 50cl	4.2	137.95	14.67
Red Stripe 24 x 50 cl	4.7	139.75	14.86
John Smith Extra Smooth 24 x 44	4.0	149.55	15.90
Newcastle Brown 24 x 50cl	4.7	150.05	15.96
Fosters 24 x 33cl	5.0	155.75	16.56
Caffreys 24 x 44cl	4.8	162.50	17.28
Holsten Pils 24 x 44cl	5.5	167.30	17.79
Kilkenny 24 x 44cl	5.0	187.05	19.89
Draught Guinness 24 x 44cl	4.1	187.50	19.94

Inter caves Wine Merchant

Inter caves

26 rue Mollien
62100 Calais
Tel: 00 33 321 96 63 82

Map Ref:	D3
Bus No:	2
English:	Yes
Tasting:	Yes
Payment:	£,
Parking:	Outside
Open:	Tuesday - Saturday 9.30am-12.30pm & 2.30-7.30pm Sunday 9.30am-12.30pm
Closed:	Monday & August

EXCLUSIVE SPECIAL OFFER:
on presentation of the Channel Hopper's Guide A magnum of Côtes du Ventoux Rouge Cuvée prestige when you spend £75 or more.

How To Get There

From the ferry terminal follow signs to Centre Ville (second exit off the roundabout). Continue straight on (railway on the right). At the end turn right into Rue Mollien. Inter caves is 200 yards along on the left hand side close to the traffic lights.

Inter caves quaintly describe themselves as 'Les Chevaliers du Vins' - The Knights of Wine! With 100 outlets around France, it seems fairly accurate.

This branch of Inter caves has a pleasant, cosy, non-rushed atmosphere. It is brightly lit and spaciously laid out. We are told that the wines are rigorously selected from hand picked individual growers and châteaux with an eye on quality. This is a typical French outlet, with an exclusively French range with prices ranging from £2.00 to £20.00.

Inter caves lay claim to being leaders in vacuumed packed bag-in-the box wines under the Réservavin label. Their selection of around 25 varieties come in 3, 10 and 20 litre tapped cartons which you are welcome to try before you buy. Ideal for parties.

Inter caves Wine Merchant

What's On Offer At Intercaves?
Prices in-store are in French Francs (FF) converted to
Sterling (£) for your convenience at a rate FF9.40 to £1.00.

Red wine boxes	FF	£
Vin de Table 10L Caves de Carpentras	110.00	11.70
Cuvée du Chevaliers 10L	125.80	13.38
Cuvée Prestige du Seigneur	171.40	18.23
Vin de Pays du Vaucluse 10L	145.50	15.48
Vin de Table Sélection 11%	149.50	15.90
Vin de Pays de la Drôme 100% Merlot	165.00	17.55
Vin de Pays d'Oc Rouge Marquise Des Vignes	172.50	18.35
Sélection Codivia (12%) 10L	172.80	18.38
Vin de Pays de Côtes du Tarn Gamay 10L	175.00	18.61
Vin de Pays du Gard 100% Cabernet 10L	179.80	19.13
Vin de Pays d'Oc rouge 100% Merlot	186.50	19.84
Costières de Nîmes AOC 10L	197.00	20.95
Côtes du Ventoux AOC 10L	199.50	21.22
Coteaux du Tricastin 13% AOC Dn du Serre Rouge	209.00	22.23
Côtes de Duras 1996 AOC	225.00	23.93
Côtes du Marmandais AOC	245.00	26.06
Bergerac AOC 10L	249.60	26.55
Côtes du Rhônes AOC - organic wine!	279.80	29.76
Bordeaux AOC 10L	315.00	33.51
Côtes de Bourg AOC 10L	349.00	37.12
Cuvée Fessy **20L**	299.80	31.89
Graves AOC 10L	349.50	38.83
Rosé wine boxes	**FF**	**£**
Vin de Pays Vaucluse 10L	155.00	16.48
Vin de Pays Gard 10L	181.00	19.25
Côtes du Ventoux AOC 10L	202.40	21.53
White wine boxes	**FF**	**£**
Vin de Pays Vaucluse 10L	155.00	16.48
Vin de Table Codivia	159.80	17.00
Côtes du Duras AOC	174.50	18.56
Bergerac Blanc sec AOC 10L	200.30	21.30

There is also an unusual and interesting selection of Champagnes
available here ranging from FF98.00 to FF369.00. Most have been
matured for three years.

Perardel
Rue Marcel Doret
Calais

Map Ref: H4
Bus No: 1 (closest)
English: A little
Tasting: Yes
Payment: £, 💳 💳
Parking: Yes
Open: 9am-7.30pm daily
Closed: -

How To Get There

Turn left out of Calais port onto the A26 motorway and exit at junction (sortie) 3. At the roundabout take the first exit signposted Zone Marcel Doret. Continue for a quarter of a mile until you see Perardel on the left hand side.

Perardel is an upmarket wine merchant with some cash & carry tendencies. The attractive premises are bright, spacious and a pleasure to peruse with wines neatly displayed on top of their boxes. There is an extensive fine wine selection with a few wines under £2.50.

There are also some Liebfraumilch and wines of similar ilk but these seem a little out of place here.

The emphasis is on good middle-range Burgundies, Clarets and white wines in £5.00-£7.50 price range. Wines from Alsace and the Loire also feature to a lesser extent. Many French 'names' and vintages are on offer and there are many fine wines in the 'sell the silver' price bracket such as Château Lafitte for around £60.00 and Château Latour for around £55.00.

If you are tentative about wine, Perardel have a computer on hand which you can use to get a description of any wine that interests you. Alternatively feel free to experiment at the small wine tasting bar.

Pidou Cash & Carry

Pidou

190 rue Marcel Dassault,
Zone Marcel Doret
62100 Calais
Tel: 00 33 3 21 96 78 10

Map Ref: H4
Bus No: 1 (closest)
English: Yes
Tasting: Yes
Payment: £,
Parking: Yes
Open: 24 hours

How To Get There

From the ferry terminal turn left onto the A26 motorway and exit at junction (sortie) 3 following the sign to ZA Marcel Doret.

Take the first left, which initially looks like a caravan site, but slightly further on is Pidou.

Pidou certainly appears to attract the bulk buyer. Its large car park is continuously laden with trucks, vans and coaches. Not surprising, since it has many attractive facilities such as a spacious car park, coffee machines, currency exchange and even a special check-out for lorry drivers.

Shopping includes a souvenir shop, groceries and sandwiches. Outside there is a chippy - installed no doubt to make the British feel at home - and a hut like construction selling a range of Belgian chocolates.
Inside there is a wide selection of mainly French wines. There are many cheap wines and included amongst them are wines with the words 'Melange de Vins de Differents pays de la Communauté Européenne'. These are not recommended for the British palate.

Pidou also have a very good range of spirits but tending to be a little expensive.

 STAR BUYS

Côtes de Provence Cellier des Garrigues FF20.20
A sound, straightforward, dryish rosé with some rough, chunky fruit.

What's On Offer At Pidou?
Quantities 75cl unless otherwise shown. Prices in-store are in French Francs (FF) converted to Sterling (£) here for your convenience at a rate FF9.4 to £1.00.

Beer	% Vol	FF	£
Blonde de Lys 24 x 25cl	4.9	30.95	3.29
Blonderbrau 20 x 25cl	4.6	31.00	3.29
Blonderbrau 24 x 25cl	4.6	32.95	3.50
Blondy 24 x 25cl	5.0	32.95	3.50
Magister 24 x 25cl	5.0	32.95	3.50
Sphinx Pils 24 x 25cl	5.0	32.95	3.50
ASB (Pidou's own) 24 x 25cl	5.2	33.95	3.61
Kirk Pils 24 x 25cl	5.0	33.95	3.61
Nordik Pils 24 x 25cl	5.0	33.95	3.61
Saint Omer 24 x 25cl	5.0	34.70	3.69
Burg Pils 24 x 25cl	5.3	34.95	3.71
Sullington 24 x 25cl	6.2	37.90	4.03
Heineken 12 x 25cl	5.0	39.80	4.23
33 Export 24 x 25cl	4.8	47.95	5.10
Kanterbrau 24 x 25cl	4.7	49.90	5.30
Nordik Gold 24 x 25cl	9.2	51.65	5.49
Stella Artois bottles 24 x 25cl	5.2	52.75	5.61
Amsterdam Mariner 24 x 33cl	5.0	52.80	5.61
Kronenbourg 20 x 25cl	4.7	53.20	5.65
Kronenbourg 26 x 25cl	4.7	56.80	6.04
Grölsch 24 x 25cl	5.0	58.80	6.25
Steel 24 x 27.5cl	6.7	63.60	6.76
Pelforth Pale 24 x 25cl	5.8	79.80	8.48
ASB (Pidou's own) 24 x 50cl	5.2	81.60	8.68
Abbaye de St Landelin 24 x 25cl	5.9	92.80	9.87
Skona Extra 24 x 50cl	8.6	96.00	10.21
Robert Cains 24 x 50cl	4.0	99.60	10.59
Dempsey's 24 x 50cl	4.8	99.70	10.60
Pelforth Brune 24 x 25cl	6.5	100.50	10.69
Stella Artois 24 x 50cl	5.2	112.80	12.00
Bombardier 24 x 50cl	4.3	123.00	13.08
Badger 24 x 50cl	4.0	127.20	13.53
Becks 24 x 33cl	5.0	127.20	13.53
Tangle Foot 24 x 50cl	5.0	130.80	13.91
Bishop's Finger 24 x 50cl	5.4	134.40	14.29
Foster's Lager 24 x 50cl	5.0	135.60	14.42

Beer contd.	% Vol	FF	£
Grölsch cans 24 x 50cl	5.0	135.60	14.42
Carling Black Label 24 x 50cl	4.1	139.20	14.80
Crest Super 24 x 50cl	10.0	142.80	15.19
Carling Premier 24 x 44cl	4.7	147.60	15.70
San Miguel 24 x 33cl	5.4	150.00	15.95
Bud 24 x 33cl	5.0	153.40	16.31
Becks 24 x 50cl	5.0	154.80	16.46
Newcastle Brown Ale 24 x 50cl	4.7	156.00	16.59
Warsteiner 24 x 50cl	4.8	156.00	16.59
Amadeus 24 x 50	4.5	168.00	17.87
Foster's Ice 24 x 33cl	5.0	171.60	18.25
Caffrey's 24 x 33cl	4.8	175.20	18.63
Holsten Pils bottles 24 x 33cl	5.5	180.00	19.14
Tennets Super 24 x 50cl	9.0	180.00	19.14
John Smith Smooth 24 x 44cl	4.0	182.60	19.42
Boddingtons 24 x 44cl	3.8	184.80	19.65
Guinness Original 24 x 44cl	4.3	187.20	19.91
Bud Ice 24 x 33cl	5.5	187.20	19.91
Budweiser 24 x 33cl	5.5	189.60	20.17
Beamish 24 x 44cl	4.2	190.80	20.29
Kestrel Super 24 x 50cl	9.0	190.80	20.29
Guinness Draught 24 x 44cl	4.1	193.20	20.55
Kilkenny 24 x 44cl	5.0	193.20	20.55
Grölsch bottles 20 x 50cl	5.0	220.00	23.40

One redeeming feature of this outlet is the staggering choice of beers which is certainly large enough to entice any passing trucker!

THE LARGEST CROSS-CHANNEL RANGE OF BEERS

Victoria Wines Cash & Carry

Victoria Wines

Unit 139, Cité Europe,
62231 Coquelles
Tel: 00 33 321 820 732

Map Ref:	A6
Bus No:	7
English:	Yes
Tasting:	No
Payment:	£, VISA mastercard
Parking:	Yes
Open:	10am to 8pm daily,
Friday	10am - 9pm,
	Saturday 10am-8pm
Closed:	Monday

How To Get There

From the port turn left and continue onto the A26. Follow the road signposted Dunkerque onto the A16. Exit at Junction (Sortie) 18 and follow signs to Boulogne. Exit at Junction (Sortie) 12. Then follow signs to Cité Europe, Centre Commercial until you get to Cité Europe. Victoria Wine is on the lower level.

A cosy outlet, nestling in the lower level of at Cité Europe close to the restaurants, opposite MacDonalds.

The biggest selection of wine is from France, followed by wines from the New World. The rest are from Eastern Europe, Iberia, Italy and Germany.

Unfortunately there are no particular facilities for dégustation (wine tasting) outside of promotional wines, but the English speaking staff are highly trained wine buffs and offer helpful and knowledgeable advice about their wines.

There is generally a good range of wines on special offer. Unfortunately due to the merger with Thresher no wines were submitted to our wine tasting. However you could try the German Slate Valley Dry Riesling - at FF20 (£2.13) - an elegant floral nose, dry crisp and clean with green apple fruit.
Others to try are Muscadet de Sèvre et Maine sur lie, Domaine de la Roulerie FF24 (£2.60), a pleasant, soft lemon example.

Vignobles & Saveurs de France

Avenue Pierre de
Coubertin
62100 Calais
Tel: 00 33 32119 30 01

Map Ref:	B3
Bus No:	-
English:	A little
Tasting:	No
Payment:	£, VISA ⬤⬤
Parking:	Yes, in front
Open:	Tuesday to Saturday 9amto 7pm Sunday 10am to 5pm
Closed:	Monday

How To Get There

From the port turn right and follow signs to Centre Ville. At the roundabout take the exit signposted Centre Ville. Continue turn right into Rue Molien. At the end of the road turn right and then first left..

The outlet is situated at the very beginning of Avenue Pierre de Coubertin.

A pretty outlet with a feeling of authenticity about it. There's a certain cellar style mustiness in the air and the stillness is broken occasionally only by the door chimes.

The outlet specialises in French wines from independent growers mainly from Languedoc-Roussillon. The rest of the 200 strong selection are from Burgundy, Rhône, Alsace and the Loire. All the wines are researched with great passion by the owner of this outlet, Dominic. He, is extremely proud of his selection. 'This is not a cash & carry' he emphasises 'all the wines proposed are quality wines direct from growers'.

Many of the growers are as yet unknown to the world at large despite their inherent quality. He believes that through his efforts he has uncovered the best in terms of quality wines at prices that have been set by the producers. In other words no profiteering middle men.

 ★ STAR BUYS ★

1996 Côtes de Brouilly, Manoir du Vernay, Claude Geoffroy FF35/£3.72
If you drink this wine immediately you will enjoy its fresh, currant aromas and fresh and fruity flavours. Very much a 'drink now' wine.

1994 Château de Jonquières, Coteaux du Languedoc FF38.00/£4.04
The aromas have quite a tang. It is sweet-edged and yet beefy too. This wine is true to its AOC, spicy, gutsy and minty.

1995 Phillippe Rageuenot, Premières Côtes de Blaye FF41.00/£4.36
This barrel fermented wine has lots of oak on the nose. The palate is rewarded with rich fruit backed by complex oak. Lots of fun and lots to get stuck into. A lush and supple wine.

1996 Château Plaisance, Côtes du Frontonnais FF28.00/£2.97
A red to chill. It gives off perfume and violets and tastes of peppered plums. A lively wine and decent value at under £3.00.

1997 Côtes Savennières les Vaults, Jessey FF42.00/£4.46
The aromas are of gentle apple scents and this gentleness follows through to the taste of soft pear fruit.

1996 Quincy, Jean-Charles Borgnat FF32.00/£3.40
A quaffable mouthful of fresh apple, grape and citrus flavours.

Wine & Beer Company

The Wine & Beer Company

Rue de Judee
ZA Marcel Doret
62100 Calais
Tel: 00 33 321 829 364

Map Ref:	H14
Bus No:	1 (closest)
English:	Yes
Tasting:	A Little
Payment:	£, VISA Mastercard
	Inhouse currency exchanged at 10FF to £1.00
Parking:	Yes
Open:	8 am to 8 pm daily
Closed:	-

BEST RANGE OF 'PARTY' WINES LESS THAN £1.00

How To Get There

From Calais follow the A26 motorway link road to the first Junction (sortie) 3. Turn left, signposted Z.A Marcel Doret (Journey time 3 minutes approximately)

From Bolougne follow the motorway (A16) to Calais, and link road, signposted Car Ferry to Junction (sortie) 3. Turn right and follow signs to ZA Marcel Doret.

The Wine and Beer Company is a British owned cash & carry and one of three in Calais. This particular branch is housed in a large warehouse style building, but without the usual chaos and dust generally associated with warehouse outlets. The Wine & Beer Company offers a spacious, well laid out and fun-themed environment in which to shop. Staff are bilingual and can advise you on the wines.

The selection consists of around 400 wines from 16 countries offering a variety of styles starting at 79p for 'party' wines.

On a recent visit Wine & Beer Company were selling Veuve Clicquot and Pol Roger Champagnes at the remarkably low prices of £13.99 and £12.99 respectively - saving a massive £9.00 each on the UK price!

Wine & Beer Company

Though Wine & Beer Company does not have the biggest selection in Calais, the beauty of this cash & carry is that if a wine tickles your palate, it will probably still be available on your next visit.

This is due to the diligence of Pat Wragg, the wine buyer. She keeps a keen eye on what the punters like and accommodates, 'because' Pat says 'taste does matter'!

 STAR BUYS ⭐

Castillo de Soldepenas, Valdepenas, Bodegas Felix Solis, £1.29
Lazy, gentle flavour of fennel and celery. Good quality at this low price.

1997 Merlot Les Soubergues, Vin de Pays d'Oc, £1.49
Delicate scents of currants, followed through with smooth currant flavours, and a fresh tarry finish. Very good value.

Wine & Beer Company

1996 Domaine de la Bouletière, Vins du Pays des Coteaux de Cabrerisse £1.69
A sharp, fresh tasting rosé. Good value at the price.

1996 Domaine des Boultières, Corbières £2.39
Clean, elegant crisp and tangy plums.

1997 Pouilly-Fumé La Bergerie, £5.69
Clean, plenty of nice mouthwatering citric acid.

1996 Château les Jacquets, Graves, £4.99
A deep coloured wine, with good depth of fruit. An elegant wine with a pebble finish.

What's On Offer At The Wine & Beer Company
Happily there have been some price reductions this year and the selection for beer has increased. If you buy 12 bottles of spirits (mixed or unmixed) you will recieve 5% discount.
In store prices are in Sterling

Sparkling wine from around the world	£
Spumante, Frizzante del Italia	0.99
Dulac,Vin Mousseaux, dry, medium and sweet	0.99
Moscato Spumante	1.29
Chardonnay Mousseux, Caves des Moines	2.69
Blanc de Blancs, Methode Traditionelle	2.99
Seppelts Great Western Brut & Rosé NV	3.49
Asti Spumanti	3.49
Saumur Brut Prestige, Methode Traditionelle	3.69
Killawarra Brut NV	3.99
Crémant de Bourgogne, Cuvée Reserve	4.49
Seaview Brut & Brut Rosé NV	4.99
Seaview Pinot Noir Chardonnay	6.99
Champagne	£
Champagne Dinet Peuvrel Brut	7.99
Rochefoucauld Vintage 1988	11.99
Joseph Perrier Brut	12.99
Pol Roger Extra Cuvee, White Foil	12.99
Charles Heidsieck Brut	13.49
Lanson Black Label Brut	13.99
Lanson Demi Sec	13.99
Joseph Perrier Brut, Magnum	23.99

Wine & Beer Company

Beer bottles by the case	% Vol	£
Pilsor 24 x 25cl	4.0%	3.79
Cristalor 24 x 25cl	4.7%	3.99
Wendlbrau 24 x 25cl	5.3%	4.29
Stella Artois 24 x 25cl	5.2%	5.29
Ruddles Best Bitter 24 x 25cl	3.7%	6.59
Kronenbourg 1664 24 x 25cl	5.2%	9.99
Kronenbourg 1664 24 x 33cl	5.2%	11.49
Becks Beer 24 x 33cl	5.0%	11.99
Old Speckled Hen 24 x 33cl	5.2%	11.99
Rolling Rock 24 x 33cl	5.0%	11.99
Labatt Ice 24 x 33cl	5.6%	11.99
Stein Lager 24 x 33cl	5.0%	12.99
Budweiser Budvar 24 x 33cl	5.0%	13.99

Canned beer & lager by the case	% Vol	£
John Bull Bitter 24 x 44cl	3.4%	8.99
Lowenbrau 24 x 50cl	4.7%	9.99
Stella Artois 24 x 50cl	5.2%	11.99
John Smiths Bitter 24 x 44cl	4.0%	11.99
Grölsch 24 x 50cl	5.0%	11.99
Ruddles Best 24 x 44cl	4.1%	12.49
Ruddles County 24 x 50cl	4.9%	12.49
Boddingtons 24 x 33cl	3.8%	12.49
Fosters 24 x 33cl	3.8%	12.49
Kronenbourg 1664 24 x 50cl	5.2%	14.49
Caffrey's Irish Ales 24 x 44cl	4.8%	15.99
Draught Guinness 24 x 44cl	4.1%	17.99

Spirits (70cl bottles unless stated)	% Vol	£
St Arbogast Creme de Cassis	15.0%	3.99
Lordson Gin	37.5%	6.59
Elstine Vodka	37.5%	6.59
Brandy 1804, 1 year old	36.0%	6.59
White Rum	37.5%	7.25
Dark Rum	37.5%	7.25
Cromwell 3 year old Scotch Whisky	40.0%	7.99
Calvados	40.0%	8.99
La Piedrecita Tequila	38.0%	8.99
Comte Josephe ***, Cognac	40.0%	9.49
Prince d'Arignac*** Armagnac	40.0%	11.99

Sherry & Port		£
Marquita Fino, Amontillado and Cream		3.99
Noval Old Coronation Ruby Port & Tawny Port both		6.99
Taylor's 1st Estate		6.99
Noval Traditional LBV 1991		9.49
Taylor's LBV 1992		9.99

Calais - Other Outlets

There are supermarkets and wine outlets galore dotted all over Calais. Below is a summary of some others.

CEDICO Supermarket
Rue Delaroche
A bright supermarket - reasonable value shopping.
Open on Sunday.

EDA Supermarket
Rue Mollien
Similar to Aldi. Very dowdy.

INTERMARCHE Supermarket
56 Ave Antoine de St Exupéry
Many Vin de Pays wines available here and general shopping is also reasonable. Particularly useful to know that Intermarché have a petrol station offering cheaper petrol and it is open on Sunday.

MATCH Supermarket
•Bvd Lafayette
•56 Place D'Armes
A stylish supermarket with a good Bordeaux selection and welcoming bakery.

PG Supermarket
• Ave Roger-Salengro
• Route St Omer
The locals shop here.

PRISUNIC Supermarket
17 Bvd Jacquard
Highly visible due to its central location, but often more expensive. If you pay in Sterling the exchange rate is a rip off, some 3 Francs less than normal. However, it is open on Sunday and if you spend 500FF or more they arrange a taxi to transport you and your shopping to the ferries or hoverport.

BWC Cash & Carry
63 Place d'Armes
Standard off licence with a range of popular products. It is situated on a busy tourist square and so prices tend to be higher.

BAR A VINS Wine Merchant
52 Place D'Armes
A quaint specialist wine shop which apparently doubles as a coffee bar but there are only two stools. The proprietor, Luc Gille, is anxious to press home the message that his stock of French wine is chosen by quality and not price - certainly no sign of Le Piat D'Or anywhere! Products include French wines from Bordeaux, Burgundy, Beaujolais, Loire, Provence, Rhône, Alsace, Vin de Pays and of course, Champagne. Prices start at £2.50.

GRAND CRU MAGNUM Cash & Carry
24 rue de Commandant Bonningu.
A specialist wine warehouse with most Bordeaux wines.

ROYAL CHAMPAGNE Specialist
9 rue André Gerschell
Tiny champagne specialist with a small selection of vintage champagnes.

LE TERROIR Wine Merchant
29 rue des Fontinettes
Small, pleasant outlet with a specialist selection of vintage and hard to find wines.

What is Cité Europe?

With representation from every European country, you instantly become an international shopper just by walking through the doors of Cité Europe!

Cité Europe is grandly located in the village of Coquelles in Calais, an area that just a few years ago - prior to the development of Eurotunnel and Cité Europe - was simply a main village road.

The name Coquelles is thought to be of Latin origin. The first Lords of Coquelles are mentioned in 1183 with Eustache de Kalquella when the village was situated near the old tower remains of the 13th century church of Old Coquelles. At that time it was just a small hamlet and since then it has had a series of European occupants: - the Romans, the English for over two centuries, the Spanish for a mere two years and the Germans for four years. How apt that Cité Europe

should be built on this very European site.

The philosophy behind Cité Europe is to bring to the shopper a truly cosmopolitan choice of shops. Each European country is represented in this immense indoor shopping centre.

Some 59,000 square metres on two levels is home to 11 major stores, including a hypermarket and 150 shops selling everything you can imagine from all over Europe. Familiar names are **The Body Shop**, **Etam**, **Tesco**, **Tie Rack**, **Toys R Us**, **Kokai** and **Naf Naf** amid others. One shop worth visiting if you like unusual candles and cristals is **Lueur d'un Soir**. On offer are candle ice creams, champagne, deserts, fruits and candle figurines and other items that they describe as *'art de la table'*.

The myriad of restaurants are just as diverse, offering everything from Sauerkraut to pizzas and hamburgers from the omnipresent MacDonalds.There's even a pub where you can enjoy a pint or two.

Some parts of the dining area are built in the style of the respective country designed to enhance the international flavour and ambience.

Leisure is also considered an important aspect of Cité Europe. With this in mind Cité Europe has a twelve screen cinema complex to accommodate all viewing preferences.

For the kids there is an adventure playground, a merry-go-round, simulators and a variety of video games.

And finally, not forgetting the wine, beers and spirits, you can enjoy a wonderful shopping day out and still go home with alcoholic bargains from Carrefour Hypermarket, Tesco Supermarket, Victoria Wines or Le Chais.

How To Get There

Cité Europe is situated opposite Eurotunnel Ideal for those travelling with Le Shuttle

From Calais port , turn left as you come out and join the A26 Autoroute. Then join the A16 Autoroute following signs to Boulogne exiting at Junction 12 (sortie 12).

Bus Route No: 7
Calais Map Ref: A6

DAY TRIPPERS BEWARE!
A visit to Cité Europe is a day trip in itself.
Once there you will find it very difficult to leave.

D940 - The Scenic Route

D940, N1, A16 - are the three different routes from Calais to Bolougne. Which do you take?

Once, the N1 was considered the main link between Calais and Boulogne. This was superseded by the A16 motorway, enabling a 20 minute dash between the two towns. Parallel to the A16 and N1 is one of the area's best kept secrets - the D940.

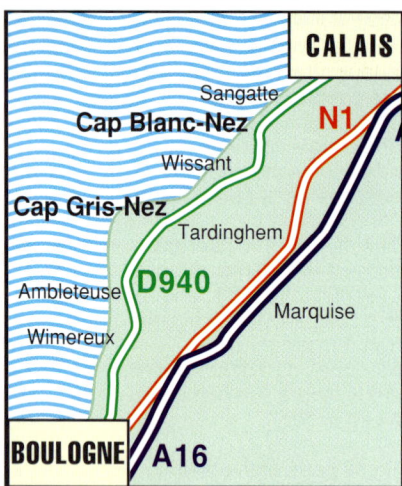

This is the scenic coastal route which ambles lazily along the Côte d'Opale. It will get you to Bolougne... eventually. Pick it up by the Calais plage (beach) signposted 'Boulogne par la Côte' and head in the direction of Sangatte. This long and winding road takes you through Bleriot Plage and over to the undulating chalk hills of the twin headlands, Cap Blanc Nez and Cap Gris Nez where swimmers taking on the Channel come ashore.

Take time-out here and make your way to their zeniths for a great visual rhapsody of untamed cliffs, the rugged greenery, the blue of the sky all reflected in the expanse of the sea.

Sandwiched between these headlands are the tiny fishing villages of Escalles and Wissant.

In Escalles there's a panoramic dining opportunity at a restaurant called Le Thomé de Gamond perched humbly on the top of Mont Hubert. If you dine here make sure you get a table by the window. Next door is the Musée de Transmanche, a museum about cross-Channel transport.

At Wissant you can see the fishermen selling their wares almost straight from the sea. Their fishing boats containing the catch of the day are hauled into the village square and they trade direct from their boats. Further along the coastal route, the beautiful fishing village of Audresselles still has its old Atlantic Wall fortifications dating from the German occupation. The fisherman here park their 'flobarts' - fishing boats - by their homes alongside their tractors. These famous flobarts are blessed every year on 15 August - a ceremony carried out in period costume.

Dotted all along the D940 route are many temptations to lure you to stop and shop. You may see farmers selling their freshly grown fruit and vegetables in open huts. These are usually located by the roadside. Or you may see signs directing you to places where you can buy fresh seafood or even flowers.

Further along, the D940 are the quaint villages of Ambleteuse and Ardinghem. Both these villages are culturally noteworthy as each has its own War Museum both of which are worth visting before continuing. Situated at the foot of Boulogne - just six miles away is Wimereux - a beautiful picture postcard seaside resort. Its sandy beaches make Wimereux popular with the French and foreign tourists alike. As well as the promenade and beach there are pretty streets with quaint cafés and shops. Wimereux is also home to Mille Vignes a quality wine merchant, specliasing in French wine.

A few sand dunes later, the D940 finally ends and Boulogne begins.......

Boulogne Town

Legend has it that in 636 AD a boat carrying only a statue of the Virgin Mary washed up on the beach of Boulogne and made it a pilgrimage site. Now they gather for the fish !

Boulogne is considered a very pleasant stopover for thousands of travellers, but those staying a little longer can enjoy the beauty, charm and heritage of this town.

The town itself is laced with quaint streets and shops and if you walk past the tidal harbour as far as the beach to the Sailor's Calvalry you will be rewarded with a good view of the port.

If you venture higher up to the old city (vieille ville) you will find the 13th century ramparts - miraculously unscathed after World War II. They surround a network of narrow cobbled streets where you can find peace from the madding crowds and enjoy a peaceful and romantic walk.

Boulogne's claim to fame is that it is France's premier fishing port - in fact a quarter of Boulogne's population are involved in fishing. Every year Boulogne celebrates its Fête du Poisson (Fish Festival) during July when 20,000 fish and seafood enthusiasts come to enjoy the grand procession led in spirit by the Virign Mary in her capacity as Patron saint of fishermen.

A major attraction is the Nausicaa national sea centre. It is only a few moments from the port with its own restaurant and multi-media library. At Nausicaa you can enjoy the wonders of the underwater world and experience the interactive terminals to the underwater observation tanks including the shark aquarium. In case all that marine watching makes you hungry, Nausicaa also has two restaurants offering anything from a sandwich to a 3 course meal.

Boulogne has its own nature reserve at the Parc Naturel Regional 'Boulonnais'. The area from the bay of Authie to the Oye beach, some 100km of coast line, is adorned with cliffs, dunes and marshes, and is preserved as a safe haven for birds and plants. Footpaths have been created for visitors and guided tours are organised to discover the national heritage.

Boulogne has its own forest spanning over 200 hectares. You can enjoy a hearty ramble through the 13 kilometres of signposted footpaths or if you prefer more exhileration, try cross-country horse riding. Alternatively you can hire a bicycle for a leisurely pedal through the countryside.

Golfers can tee off at no less than three 18 hole golf courses; one at Wimereux and two in Hardelot.

Perhaps, a little shopping at one of the hypermarkets followed by a relaxing drink and croissant is more your style. If so, you will be pleased with the myriad of restaurants and continental style cafés Boulogne has to offer.

Leisure in Boulogne
Nausicaa Centre National de la Mer Boulevard Sainte-Beuve Open daily - 10am-6pm. Located just minutes from Seacat.
Tel: (00 33) 3 21 30 99 99

Parc naturel régional du Boulonnais Maison du Parc à le Wast
Tel: (00 33) 3 21 83 38 79

Golf - (all 18 holes)
Golf de Wimereux, route d'Ambleteuse, Wimereux
Tel: (00 33) 3 21 32 43 20
Golf des Pins
avenue de Golf, Hardelot
Tel: (00 33) 3 21 83 73 10
Golf des Dunes
avenue Edouard VII Hardelot
Tel: (00 33) 3 21 91 90 90

Horse Riding Centre Équestre du Boulonnais
Tel: (00 33) 3 21 83 32 38

Bicycle Hire
Youth Hotel, Rue Porte Gayole
Tel: (00 33) 3 21 83 32 59

Fish Market
Quai Gambetta Mon. to Sat. mornings. Opposite SeaCat Port.

General Market Days
Place Dalton. All day Wed & Sat

Sea Fishing
Fishing Club Boulonnais, 3 rue Coquelin, Boulogne
Tel: (00 33) 3 21 87 55 99

**Touristic brochures applaud the charm
and beauty of Boulogne,
but is it just a pretty face?**

Hôtel de Ville,
Place de la Résistance

The town hall has been altered six times since it was restored in the 18th century. It houses oil portrait paintings and the Wedding Room contains wood carvings from Dutch Oak.

Château-Museé
rue de Bernet

There is so much to see in this mediaeval Château Museum you may well run out of time. It was originally built by the Count of Boulogne and his wife Mahaut, and now you can walk through the vaults and underground passages of this listed building. In the museum you can enjoy 4,000m2 of antique Grecian vases, Egyptian sarcophogi, renaissance coins, Eskimo and Aleutian masks and many exhibits brought back from Oceania 100 years ago by the sailors of Boulogne.

Le Beffroi

(attached to the Town Hall) The bellfry is the oldest monument in the Old Town. It was once used as a dungeon and symbolises communal liberty. It is worth visiting if only for the breath-taking views of the port, the town and the sea. Access is from the ground floor of the town hall. Entrance is free.

Basilique Notre-Dame,
Enc de l'Evêche

This 'hybrid' cathedral was collectively inspired by St Paul's Cathedral, St Peter's in Rome, the Panthéon and Les Invalides in Paris.

It is located on top of a 12th century maze of crypts and its dome dominates Boulogne town. It has 14 chambers containing vestiges of the 3rd century Roman temple and many bejewelled religious artifacts.

Les Remparts

Did you know that Boulogne is a walled city? Not many do. The 13th century fortifications surround the cobbled streets of the Haute Ville. Built by the Count of Boulogne on the foundations of a Gallo-Roman wall, it has four gates and seventeen turrets. Take a peaceful stroll along the ramparts to enjoy the panoramic views of the town and its coastline.

Le Bellfroi

The Cathedral Dome dominates the town of Boulogne

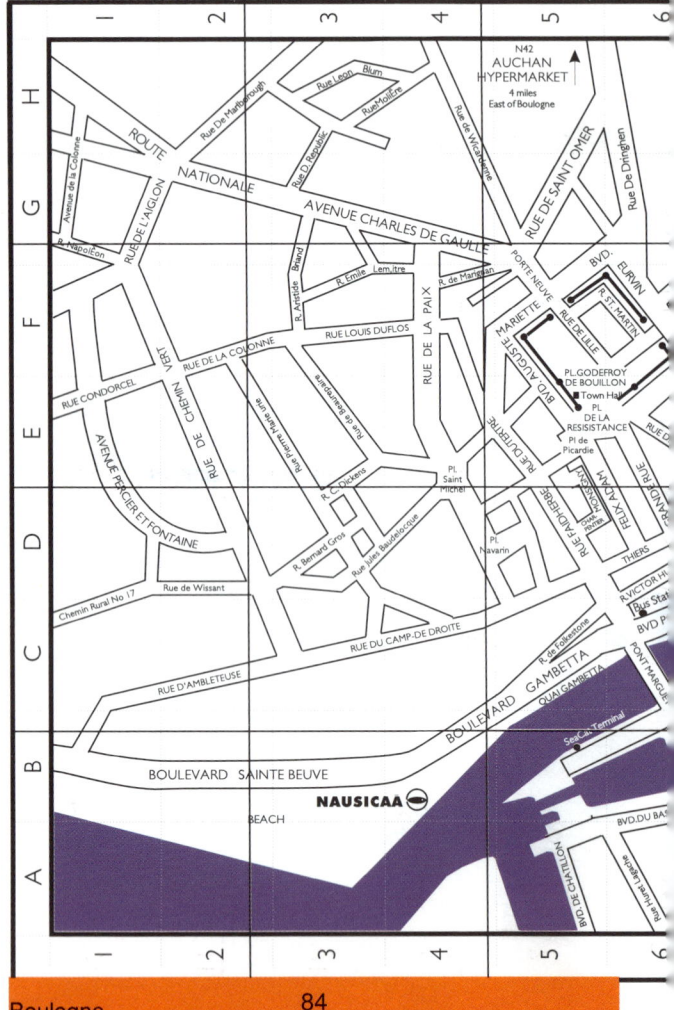

BEACH

NAUSICAA ⊕

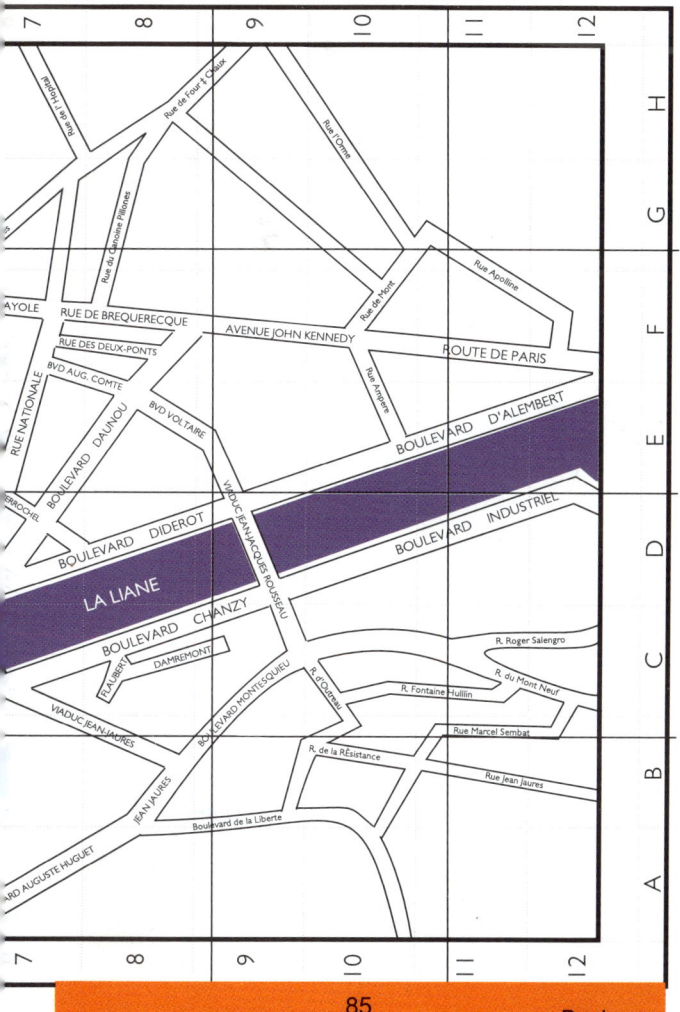

Boulogne

Auchan Hypermarket

Auchan
RN42
6220 St-Martin Boulogne

Map Ref:	Follow H5 direction
Bus No:	8
English:	No
Tasting:	No
Payment:	£, VISA, Mastercard
Parking:	Yes
Open:	Monday to Saturday 8.30am to 10pm
Closed:	Sunday

BEST HYPERMARKET GROUP

How To Get There

From the port of Boulogne initially follow signs to St Omer and St Martin-B then signs for St Martin B-Centre. Follow the N42 straight through the town on the Route de St Omer and cross over the roundabout with MacDonalds on the right. Cross over the next roundabout too, continue for 1.5 miles, take the exit Centre Commercial direct to Auchan and follow signs to Centre Commercial. Auchan will loom up ahead of you.

Auchan Hypermarket is generally considered the biggest and the best place to visit in Boulogne for general supermarket shopping. It is brightly lit, very spacious, and very colourful.

Together with its sister branch in Calais, Auchan has won the Best Hypermarket Group for its breadth of products and competitive pricing.

As is typical of French hypermarkets, Auchan dominates a shopping complex housing many small retail shops and service outlets.

For detailed product listings and recommendations , please see the entry for Auchan in the Calais section.

For a list of spirits please refer to the Tipple Table.

Centre E. Leclerc
Boulevard Industrial
de la Liane,
62230 Outreau

Map Ref: D12
Bus No: 22
English: No
Tasting: No
Payment: £, VISA ●●
Parking: Yes
Open: Monday to Saturday
            9am to 8pm
Closed: Sunday

How To Get There

From the port turn immediate right and follow the signs to Z I de la Liane on Boulevard Chanzy (alongside the canal on the left).

Continue for about a quarter of a mile and Centre E. Leclerc is on the right hand side.

We like to refer to this supermarket as 'baby Auchan'. It is bright and spacious and similar in many ways to Auchan from its decor to the products and even prices. More than Auchan, Leclerc has a reputation for economoy lines and value-for-money.

However its smaller size means it is a far more intimate place to shop. A small section of the supermarket has been designed to look like a cellar complete with dimmed lighting - not surprisingly it is called 'La Cave'. It is here that the quality wines are kept. These are exclusively French quality wines, Champagnes and quality liqueurs.

There are some wines from other countries too but they are kept on the shelves in the main shop with the cheaper French plonk!

Le Chais Cash & Carry

Le Chais

Bréquercque Village,
49 rue des Deux Ponts
Boulogne

Map Ref:	F8
Bus No:	9 & 14 (stop close by)
English:	A little
Tasting:	Some
Payment:	£, VISA ●
Parking:	Yes
Open:	9am-7pm
Closed:	12pm-2.30pm each day & all day Sunday and Monday

How To Get There

From the Boulogne port cross over the bridge and veer right at the lights. Continue straight on (Boulevard Dannau).

At the lights (BP on the right) continue into Boulevard Beaucerf and take the first left turning. Le Chais is on the right hand side.

Underneath the arches of Boulogne's railway station is Le Chais, a large warehouse style cash and carry.

As is typical of French owned wine outlets, the range of wines is predominantly French. The selection is larger than that of the Calais branch. Wines are generally sold in boxes of six or by the mixed dozen with incentives of free wines with bulk purchases.

Le Chais describe themselves as, 'A cellar for those who appreciate fine wines'. With the majority of wines at around £4.00 or over and with names such as Jaboulet, Jadot and Chapoutier jostling for attention, this would be an apt description.

Cave Paul Herpe

85 rue Pasteur, St Martin
Boulogne
Tel 00 33 3468 42 52 20

Map Ref: Follow H5 direction
Bus No: 9
English: Not much
Tasting: En vrac
Payment: £,
Parking: Yes
Open: 9am-12.15pm & 2pm-
            7pm daily
Closed: Sunday

How To Get There

From Boulogne port follow signs to St. Omer and St. Martin- B. Follow the N42 straight through the town on the Route de St Omer.

Turn left into Rue de la Colonne and then take 3rd right into Rue Pasteur.

This outlet specialises in the wines of just one region of France - the Languedoc. Here you can discover the delights of this Southern area of France. There's a selection too that can be bought en vrac. The wine is contained in huge cylinders and dispensed into containers. Prices start at £1.50 for vins de table to £2.75 per litre for an AOC Corbières, Minervois or Fitou.

★ STAR BUYS ★

1996 Château des Frigoulières, Corbières FF28.50

Slightly herbaceous nose. Soft, tangy but a little green

1997 Château Auris White, Corbières FF30.50

Fennel on the nose, intense, quite bright acidity, fresh and clean.

1997 Château Auris Rosé, Corbières FF25.50

An orange-pink hue, not much scent though. It is soft, tangy and quite dry.

1996 Ibid red FF26.50

A light easy drinking wine. Soft, sound and satisfying.

Muscat de Riversaltes. 'En vrac' FF42.00 per litre per 75cl bottle FF38.00

You can buy this sweet fortified wine that the Languedoc was originally famous for, en vrac.

The Grape Shop
The Seacat Port
Boulogne
Tel: 00 33 3 21 30 80 45

Map Ref: B5
English: Yes
Tasting: Yes
Payment: £,
Parking: Yes
Open: 9am-9pm daily
Closed: -

The Grape Shop nestles unobtrusively but conveniently within the Seacat port. This is ideal for foot passengers who can benefit from the Select & Collect service - make your purchases and then collect them in Folkestone upon your return leaving you free to enjoy Boulogne unencumbered. Unfortunately The Grape Shop were still compiling their new portfolio of wines and so were unable to paticipate in our wine

How To Get There
The outlet is situated in the Seacat port.

tasting. The wine buying team headed by Nick Davies (pictured below) have been hard at work tasting over 1000 wines from around the world. However the following are some old faithfuls:

☆ STAR BUYS ☆

1996 Richemont Cabernet Sauvignon Reserve, Vin de Pays d'Oc FF26.00
A good solid vins de pays, with dusty warmth to it. It is chewy, rich and full of tannins.

1995 Merlot, Richemont Ibid FF26.00
Sweet and clean on the nose. To taste it has spicy fruit with a sweet edge. Plummy and fresh.

Mille Vignes Wine Merchant

Mille Vignes

90 Rue Carnot, 62930
Wimereux
Tel: 00 33 321 32 60 13

Map Ref:	follow B1
Bus No:	-
English:	Yes
Tasting:	Yes
Payment:	VISA ● & FF only
Parking:	Opposite the shop and off street
Open:	Tuesday - Saturday 10am-1.30pm & 2.30-7.00pm Sunday 10am-1pm
Closed:	Monday

How To Get There

From Calais port Take the A6/A26 motorway towards Boulogne - Turn off at Junction 4-Wimilles/ Wimereux Nord. Follow signs for Centre of Wimereux.

From Boulogne port: Turn left, then left again, past Nausicaa, and take D940 coast road in the direction of Wimereux/ Calais.

BEST FRENCH WINE OUTLET IN BOULOGNE

The owner of Mille Vignes, is an Englishman with a palate, it seems, for fine French wine. It was through this passion that the idea of a wine outlet in France selling quality French wines to the English was created.

Mille Vignes, a cosy, corner outlet, was opened by the Mayor of Wimereux two years ago. The owner, a silversmith by trade and currently working in England, leaves the management of Mille Vignes to Nick Sweet. Nick is another Englishman and a connoisseur of wines with a long history in wine. Nick is very approachable and is happy to guide you through the selection.

The speciality is French wines from the Rhône, Loire, white Burgundy, Claret originating from family owned Domaines and Châteaux. Amid their consistently good selection there are many wines to recommend.

 ★ STAR BUYS ★

1997 Syrah Rosé, Domaine de Montpezat Vin de Pays d'Oc 25FF/£2.65
Fair quality French rosé, deep and long.

1996 Corbières, Château La Boutignane, 23FF/£2.44
Though not subtle, this wine is a challenging, lively wine, herbaceous in style. Deep and long with depth and decent guts.

1996 St Chinian, Château Viranel 33FF/£3.51
Nice floral, vegetal scents, full, perfumed, deep, sprightly, lots of viivd depth. A great wine.

1996 Rasteau, Côtes du Rhône Domaine St Gayan 39FF/£4.14
Softy and spicy, with a long savoury dry-spice finish.

1995 Fronsac, Château Puy-Guilhem 65FF/£6.91
Chewy, meaty flavours with sturdy tannins.

1996 Le Vieux Donjon, Châteauneuf du Pape 89FF/£9.46
Fresh, floral scents, bright pungent fruit. Good for those with a taste for zing!

Mille Vignes

Champagne Charlies ?

Are the Brits perceived as Champagne Charlies?
Duty on Champagne is a mere £1.50.
So why is the price so much higher in the UK?

If you love Champagne then here is some good news to raise your spirits. For some mysterious reason Champagne can be anything up to half price in France.

It is not uncommon to buy non-vintage lessor known brands of Champagne for the astonishingly low price of between £6-£9 in the hypermarkets.

Auchan, for instance, have one example - Philippe de Nantheuil Brut - at just £5.53. What is going on? You may well ask.

As long as the status quo remains, Champagne represents a fantastic bargain across the Channel and you may as well stock up now for the millenium while stocks and prices are in place.

Champagnes at the French Supermarkets					
Champagne	Average £ UK	Tesco £	Auchan £	Carrefour £	Continent £
Canard Duchêne	15.49	10.16	10.99	10.10	
Lanson Black Label	18.99	14.31	11.67	11.67	
Laurent Perrier	20.99	12.91	12.62	12.68	
Mercier Brut	16.99	11.13	9.35	10.62	
Moët et Chandon	19.99	13.42	15.31	13.49	
Mumm Cordon Rouge	18.49	13.15	12.26	12.76	
Nicolas Feuillate		9.43	8.24	8.74	
Piper Heidsick	18.99			12.30	11.70
Taittinger	22.99				12.68
Veuve Clicquot Ponsardin	22.99		14.35	14.34	

That's The Spirit - The Tipple Table

Head for the hypermarkets if you really want good value spirits. Other outlets just cannot compete. The following table lists 100 of the most popular products in alphabetical order. Where possible we have included the average UK price so that you can see your savings at a glance. Prices have been converted to Sterling for your convenience. Prices tend to fluctuate, usually within a 5% band. The table that follows is a guide to what you can expect. TIPPLE TABLE - PRICES ARE IN £ STERLING

PRODUCT	% vol	Average UK price	Tesco	Auchan	Carrefour	Continet
Aberlour Scotch Whisky 10yrs 70cl	43	18.49	12.19	12.50	12.09	12.09
Absolut Vodka 70cl	40			9.03	9.10	9.03
Bacardi White Rum 1L *70cl	37.5	15.39	10.48	*7.92	*7.93	
Baileys Irish Cream 1L *70cl	17	16.95	13.25	*7.86		
Ballantines 70cl	40			8.61	81.61	8.64
Beefeater London Dry Gin 70cl	40	12.44		8.28		8.19
Bells 8yrs 70cl	40	11.99		8.90		8.90
Benedictine 70cl	40	16.99		10.58	10.61	
Black & White Scotch Whisky 70cl	40			7.78	7.73	7.71
Bombay Sapphire London Dry Gin 70cl	40	12.99	9.54	13.82		11.15
Calvados 70cl	40				8.44	
Campari 1L	25			8.46	8.44	8.46
Canadian Club Whisky 70c	40	14.18	9.69	7.61	7.61	10.63
Canadian Mist Whisky 70cl	40			7.12	7.13	7.02
Captain Morgan 1L	40	16.99	10.59			
Cardhu Single Malt 70cl	40	17.22				16.42
Chivas Regal Scotch Whisky 12 yrs 70cl	40			15.02	14.88	14.78
Cinzano Bianco 1L *75cl	16	*4.99		4.25		4.03
Cinzano Rosso 1L	16			4.03	4.02	4.03
Clan Campbell 1L	40			10.63	10.36	10.36
Cles Des Ducs Armagnac 70cl	40				8.86	8.86
Cognac Bisquit Classique 70cl	40					11.69
Cointreau 70cl	40	16.18	13.67	10.07	10.07	9.58
Courvoisier Cognac 70cl	40	20.34		17.43		
Croft Tawny Port 75cl	19.5			5.40		
Cutty Sark Scotch Whisky 70cl	40			8.37	8.37	8.33
Dimple 70cl	40			16.95	15.78	17.19
Dramuie 70cl	40	17.99	15.80			
Dubonnet 1L	16	7.48		4.77	4.88	4.77

94

That's The Spirit

PRODUCT	% vol	Average UK price	Tesco	Auchan	Carrefour	Continet
Eristoff Vodka 70cl	37.5				6.89	6.26
Famous Grouse Scotch Whisky 70cl	40.0			10.94		9.27
Four Roses Bourbon Scotch Whisky 70cl	40.0			9.40	9.40	9.75
Gilbey's London Dry Gin 70cl	37.5			6.22	6.02	6.16
Glen Rogers Scotch Whisky 8yrs 70cl	40.0			8.86	8.88	8.66
Glen Turner Pure Malt 8yrs 70cl	40.0			9.08	9.12	9.13
Glenfiddich 70cl	40.0	21.10	19.49	13.04	13.00	15.15
Glenlivet 12 yrs 70cl	40.0	19.99	14.31	15.95	15.42	
Glenmorangie 10yrs 70cl	40.0	22.99	17.92	17.72		17.66
Gold River 8yrs 70cl	30.0					
Gordon's London Dry Gin 1L *70cl	37.5	14.79			6.53	10.59
Grand Marnier Liqueur 70cl	40.0	18.18	15.80	10.80	*6.98	8.79
Grants Whisky 70cl *1L	40.0	10.15		7.31	10.80	*10.20
Haig Gold Label 70cl	40.0				7.28	
Harveys Bristol Cream 1L	17.5	7.89	7.31		6.97	
Hennessy Cognac 1L *70cl	40.0					*12.78
J&B Whisky 70c	40.0			9.46	20.65	9.46
Jack Daniels Whisky 70cl	43.0	17.29	11.66	12.00		11.34
Jameson Irish Whiskey 70cl	40.0	11.99		9.39	9.37	9.37
Janneau Grand Armagnac 1L * 70cl	40.0	*9.44		12.36		
Jim Bean Bourbon 70cl	40.0	15.23	10.47			9.24
Johnnie Walker Black Label 70cl	40.0					13.32
Johnnie Walker Red Label 1L *70cl	40.0	14.33		11.61	11.60	11.99
Kahlua Liqueur 70cl	26.0	12.69	10.49	8.45		8.45
Knockando Whisky 70cl	43.0	18.33		16.80		16.90
Label 5 70cl	40.0			7.26	7.25	
Lambs Navy Rum 70cl	40.0	10.79				
Laphroaig 70cl	43.0	21.99				19.57
Laphroig 10 yrs 70cl	40.0			7.17	9.46	7.17
Long John Scotch Whisky 70cl	40.0					
Macallan 70cl	43.0				21.17	21.17
MacArthur's 70cl	40.0					
Malibu White Rum 1L	21.0	11.29	8.37	6.62	6.22	6.37

That's The Spirit - The Tipple Table

PRODUCT	% vol	Average UK price	Tesco	Auchan	Carrefour	Continet
Martell 3 Star Cognac 70cl	40.0	25.49	16.86			
Martini Bianco 1L	16.0	5.99	4.97	4.77	4.68	4.79
Martini Rosé 1L	16.0	5.99	4.94	4.81	4.77	4.77
Martini Rosso 1L	16.0	5.99	4.94	5.07	4.68	4.79
Muscat Riversaltes 1L	15.5					2.47
Negrita Rum 1L	40.0			7.19	7.17	7.19
Noilly Prat 1L *75cl	18.0	*5.99	*5.29	5.50	5.49	5.50
Old Lady's London Dry Gin 70cl	37.5			5.31	6.29	
Old Nick White Rum 70cl	40.0				5.30	
Old Virginia Bourbon 70cl *1L	40.0				*12.23	
Pastis 51 1L *70cl	45.0			7.89	*7.38	7.91
Pernod 1L *75cl	15.0	13.99	11.55	10.31	10.58	10.55
Pimms 70cl	25.0	11.99	10.49		10.58	10.59
Remy Martin VSOP 70cl	40.0	26.18	20.04			
Ricard Pastis 70cl	45.0				7.18	7.18
Rozés Tawny Porto 75cl	20.0			10.49	10.50	
Sandeman Port 75cl	19.0			5.56	5.56	
Smirnoff Vodka 70cl	37.5	13.99	13.35	6.92		6.92
St James White Rum 70CL	40.0			7.33	6.80	6.93
Southern Comfort 70cl	40.0	14.99	11.75	10.12	10.12	
Stones Original Ginger Wine 70cl	n/a	5.19	4.69			
Teachers Scotch Whisky 70cl	40.0	11.69	8.87		7.90	7.49
Tia Maria 70cl *50	26.5	13.99	12.61	*6.90	9.35	
Vladivar Vodka 1L	37.5	13.64	8.64			
Warninks Advocaat 70cl	17.2	9.99	7.66			
White Horse Scotch Whisky 70cl	40.0	10.99	8.37			7.60
Whyte & Mackay Special Reserve 70cl	40.0	11.29	8.50	9.59	9.56	8.23
Wild Turkey No.8 Bourbon Whisky 70cl	43.4			7.61	7.97	9.58
William Lawson Scotch Whisky 70cl *L	40.0					*10.52
William Peel 1L *70cl	40.0			10.02	10.02	*6.86
Wyborowa Vodka 70cl	40.0					
Zubrowka Vodka 70cl	40.0			8.81	8.79	8.76

France is one of the leading wine producing countries and this is reflected in the French outlets where most, if not all, of their selection is French. With so much choice, it helps to know a little about French wine.

Firstly, inspect the label for an indication and therefore an assurance of the quality of the wine. The best wines of the regions have Appéllation Contrôlées on the label which gives a guarantee of the origin, supervision of production method, variety of grape and quantity produced.

Less controlled but still good value wines , are listed as Vins Délimités de Qualité Supérieure (VDQS) and are worth trying. There are also the Vins de Pays. These are country wines, more widely found in the South of France, which do not specify the exact location of the vineyard but are generally worth a try and often offer the best value for money. Good examples are Vin de Pays du Gard and the wines from Côtes de Gascogne. Further down the ladder are the Vins de Table. They are varied in quality but are so cheap that they are worth a gamble. You could be surprised for as little at FF5-12.00 (55p-£1.33).

We have very broadly categorised the wine growing areas into seven major regions.
These are: Alsace, Burgundy, Bordeaux, Champagne, Loire, Midi and Rhône.

Which Wine?

Alsace

The Alsace is situated in Eastern France on the German border.

The wine labels from this area differ from the rest of France by calling the wine by the name of the grape rather than the area e.g. Gewürztraminer, Riesling.

If a label reads Alsace AC, this is the standard Alsace wine which is typically Germanic in character, often being aromatic and fruity, but drier than its German equivalent.

A label with Alsace Grand Cru printed on it indicates a higher quality and only the four most highly regarded grape types can be used in its making and they are: Gewürztraminer, Riesling (not to be confused with the German wine of the same name), Tokay Pinot and Muscat. These are medium priced white wines with reliable quality and are generally dry to medium dry. The Alsation wines are great aperitifs and also combine well with fish, poultry, salads or with a summer meal.

Expect to pay: 15-30 francs (£1.66-£3.33) per bottle.

Bordeaux

Bordeaux is in the South West region of France with the Dordogne region on its eastern border and the Atlantic ocean on the west.

The term Claret refers to the red dry wines of this region and wines such as Médoc, St. Emillion and Pomerol which are in the lower price range.

There are also numerous wines known by the name of Château. Quality, especially at the lower end, can be variable. Claret goes well with meat, chicken and cheese.

Expect to pay: From as little as 14 francs (£1.55) per bottle, to more than 100 francs (£12.50) for a top class Château.

Situated between Bordeaux and the Dordogne valley is an area called Bergerac.

Bergerac has a complete range of wines of its own; most commonly Bergerac (red, rosé and dry white), Côtes de Bergerac (red and medium sweet wine), Monbazillac (sweet white) and Pécharmant (fine red).

Expect to pay: 10-16 francs (£1.11-£1.77) for the Bergerac. 30 francs (£3.33) for Monbazillac.

Burgundy

Burgundy is an area of France south-east of Paris running from Chablis at the northern end, down through to Lyon at the southern end. About 75% of the wine production in this region is red with the remainder white.

It is worth noting the area on the label when choosing a Burgundy wine since the more exact the area, the finer the wine is likely to be. The best are labelled 'Grand Cru',followed by 'Premier Cru', 'Villages', a specified region and finally, the most basic will have just Burgundy. The best known of the whites is Chablis which is in the higher price bracket. The Côte de Beaune produces some of the finest such as Meursault and some good light dry wines come from Mâconnais such as Mâcon Blanc and Pouilly Fuissé. All Burgundy white wines are dry and are an ideal accompaniment for fish.

The finest red Burgundy wine comes from the Côtes de Nuits such as Nuits St Georges and the Côtes de Beaune namely Pommard, Volnay and Monthélie. These are best drunk with meat, game and cheese.

Expect to pay: 35-70 francs (£3.88-£7.77) These wines tend to be reliable in this price bracket.

Best known of the reds in the South of this region is

Beaujolais. Beaujolais is divided into the standard Beaujolais AC, Beaujolais Superieur which denotes a slightly higher alcohol content and Beaujolais-Villages which is an appéllation controllée (quality control) given to about 40 villages and considered to be of superior quality

The most prestigious of the Beaujolais wines bear the name of one of the ten communes (Crus). These are worth noting since you will come across them practically everywhere. These are Saint-Amour, Juliénas, Chénas, Moulin-à-Vent, Fleurie, Chiroubles, Morgon, Brouilly, Côte de Brouilly and Régnié (the most recently created, but least distinguished Cru).

These are medium priced red dry fruity wines with the Villages and Communes especially reliable and should be drunk young and served slightly chilled.

Expect to pay: 10-25 francs (£1.11-£2.77) for basic Beaujolais AC. 15-45 francs (£1.87-£5.62) per bottle for Beaujolais- Villages or named Commune.

Midi
(Languedoc Roussillon & Provence)
This region stretches from north east of Marseilles down to the west of Perpignan bordering Spain.

Wines from this region, such as Minervois and Corbières represent good value dry reds. The Vin de Pays (sometimes referred to as Country Wines) of the area offer the best value of all. The label will always show the Vin de Pays description followed by the region.

Expect to pay: 6-20 francs (66p-£2.22) per bottle and a little more if VDQS (Vins Délimités de Qualité Supérieure) is printed on the label.

Rhône

This area is located south of the Burgundy region and continues due south to the Mediterranean near Marseilles. The region generally produces robust, full bodied wines.

There is the standard Côtes du Rhône and the Côtes du Rhône Villages which is famous for its dry red wine. If the wine is attributable to a named village (which is shown on the label) the chances are it will be better quality but naturally more expensive. Côtes du Rhône wines accompany cheese and poultry dishes very well.

Expect to pay: 8-20 francs (88p-£2.22) for Côtes du Rhône label wines. 20-30 francs (£2.22-£3.33) for Côtes du Rhône Villages.

Loire

The Loire wine region starts at Nantes on the Western Atlantic coast of France and follows the Loire river east to Orléans where it cuts back southeast to Sancerre. The majority of wines produced in this area are white.

The Loire offers the widest variety of wine of any area in France and all have a certain refreshing quality that comes from the northerly position of most of the major Loire vineyards and the character of the soil.

Amongst the many well-known names from this area are Muscadet, Gros Plant Du Nantais, Pouilly-Fumé and Sancerre being examples of dry whites, and Anjou which is well known for its Rosé.

The Rosé wine is very versatile and can be drunk throughout the course of the meal. The whites are best with fish and salads.

Although named wines are generally a better buy, in our experience it is especially true for Muscadet where we recommend either a named or 'sur lie' over the ordinary Muscadet.

Expect to pay: 8-15 francs (88p-£1.66) for Gros Plant. 10-22 francs (£1.11-£2.44) for Muscadet. 35-39 francs (£3.88-£4.33) for Sancerre & Pouilly Fumé 10-16 francs (£1.11-£1.77) for Anjou Rosé wines.

If you prefer a medium dry wine then try the Vouvray at 20-25 francs (£2.50-£3.12). Vouvray is also available as a sparkling wine.

Champagne

'I am drinking stars'
Dom Perignon describing his sparkling wine

The most luxurious drink in the world, sparkling wine, suggests celebration - something special. Situated north east of Paris with Reims and Epernay at the heart Champagne is renowned for sparkling wine. The climate, the soil, the art of the wine maker and of course the grapes all combine to make champagne the most celebrated in terms of unmatched quality and reputation. These are usually sold under a brand name e.g. Bollinger, Moët et Chandon, Mumm, Veuve Clicquot etc. which are nearly always dry. If you do not like dry wines, then ask for a demi-sec or even a rosé Champagne. Only wine made in the champagne area is entitled to be called Champagne. Other wine of this type is referred to as 'sparkling' wine but some have Méthode Traditionelle on the label which means made in the Champagne method'.

Expect to pay: 56-70 francs (£5.90-£7.77) for lesser known brands. 115 francs (£12.77) upwards for well-known brands.

Without a doubt, the best bargain to be had in France is the beer. With savings of up to 50 per cent, beer drinkers are certainly not bitter !

Fortunately, beer is in abundance in Calais and Boulogne and the most widely available beers tend to be continental. The average continental beer has an alcoholic content of at least 4.5% which is more than 1% stronger than the average British bitter.

You may find 'promos' offering beers cheaply but these could be lower alcohol beers such as Kœnigsbier or Brandeberg which both retail at around £2.80 for 24 bottles but both have an alcoholic volume of only 2.80%!

The majority of continental beers are light in colour and are best served chilled. These are sold in 25cl bottles which equates to just under half a pint (0.43).

The highest alcoholic beers tend to be from Belgium. The more popular ones include Hoegaarden (5% ABV) known as Witbier or

Bière Blanche meaning White Beer and refers to its naturally cloudy appearance. Although in Britain cloudiness is usually associated with the beer being past its best, in this case, it is due to its production process and ingredients: barley, unmalted wheat, Styrian and Kent hops, coriander and curacao. As it brews, the top-fermenting yeast turns the malt to alcohol, but because the wheat is not malted, the starches contribute to the final cloudy appearance.

Possibly the best-known Belgium beers are Trappist beers made by monks in just 5 Trappist monastery breweries in Belgium. These include Chimay Red (7%) - copper colour and slightly sweet, Chimay White (6.3%) - lots of hop and slightly acidic, Chimay Blue (7.1%) - fruity aromas, Orval (6.2%) - orange hue,with acidity;

Here For The Beer?

Rochefort 6,8,10 (ABVs are 7.3%, 7.5% and 11.3%) - characteristics range from russet colour with a herbal palate, tawny and fruity to dark brown with chocolate and fruity palate respectively.

Pilsner style beers include the mass marketed beers of Jupiler, a dry and soft easy drinking beer and Stella Artois (the biggest brewing company in Belgium) who also make Leffe - an abbey style ale.

France itself has two brewing regions. The first is in the North around the city of Lille, the most well known part being French Flanders. The style of beer produced - bière de garde - resembles its Belgian counterparts. Strasbourg, in the East is the other brewing region. The final product is similar to German lagers.

The major French breweries are Kronenbourg/Kanterbrau, Mutzig and Pelforth. The latter situated near Lille and owned by Heineken, produces light and dark lagers: Pelforth Blonde (5.8%) and Pelforth Brune (5.2% & 6.5%).

There are also popular beers from 'down under' such as Castlemain XXXX and the sweetish Fosters lager (both 4%) which are widely availabe.

Products from many British breweries also share shelf space in Northern France, especially at British supermarkets such as Tesco.These include Shepherd Neame's malty Bishop's Finger (12.5%), John Smith's bitter (4.8% & 4%), Whitbread's creamy headed Boddington's bitter (3.8%), Tetley's creamy, nutty Yorkshire ale (3.6%) and Ireland's earthy, dry Guinness Draught (5%).

Whichever beer you choose your enjoyment will be heightened by the knowledge that it often costs only half of what you would have paid in the UK ! Cheers.

Here For The Beer?

Yes, it true ! Beer from 11p Per 25cl Bottle !!!

Beer	% Vol	£p	Outlet
Belzebuth	5.0	11	Beer Lovers
Helbrau	2.8	11	Auchan
Koenigbier	2.6	11	Continent
Alsabrau	4.5	12	Carrefour
Alsa Brun	4.5	12	Carrefour
Koenigbier	3.7	12	Continent
Masbräu	4.5	12	Boozers
Norvilland	4.0	12	Auchan
Biere du Lux	n/a	13	Tesco
Lovers Beer	5.1	13	Beer Lovers
Alsace Lager	n/a	14	Tesco
Amos	4.8	14	Boozers
Blonde de Lys	4.9	14	Pidou
Marten's	5.0	14	Beer Lovers
Umberland	4.5	14	Eastenders
Burg Pils	5.3	15	Pidou
ASB	5.2	15	Pidou
Blondy	5.0	15	Pidou
Nordheim	4.7	15.	Le Chais
Magister	5.0	15	Pidou
Sphinx Pils	5.0	15	Pidou
Bière Blonde	4.6	15	Carrefour
Bruckbier Blonde	4.7	15	Continent
Kirk Pils	5.0	15	Pidou
Maltson Pils	n/a	15	Franglais
Nordik Pils	5.0	15	Pidou
Classic	5.0	16	Eastenders
Blonderbrau	4.6	16	Pidou
Cristalor	4.7	16	Wine&Beer Co
Artenbrau	5.0	16	Carrefour
Sterling	4.9	16	Auchan
Pilsor	4.0	16	Wine&Beer Co
Upsthem	5.2	15	Le Chais
ESP	5.2	17	Eastenders
La Facon Blonde	4.9	17	Auchan/Carrefour/Continent
Sullington	6.2	17	Pidou
St. Omer	5.0	15	Pidou/Tesco/Franglais
Amsterdam Mariner	5.0	18	Beer Lovers
Kanterbrau	4.7	18	Continent
33 Export	4.8	18	Carrefour/Continent/Auchan
Wendlbrau	5.3	18	Wine&Beer Co
Meteor	4.6	19	Auchan
Semeuse	4.7	19	Carrefour
Pelforth Blonde	5.8	20	Auchan
Kronenbourg	4.7	21	Carrefour/Continent
Alsatia	5.1	21	Beer Lovers
Stella Artois	5.2	21	Eastenders

Here For The Beer?

Beer Labels
What you see on a beer label is what you get. But what do the terms mean?

Abbey, Abbaye: This suggests a beer made by monks - not so, but the trappist style has been used. Sometimes an abbey will have licensed it.

Ale: An English word meaning a brew made with a top-fermenting yeast - expect a certain fruitiness to its flavour

Bière de Gard: A French phrase for a top-fermented brew with an alcohol content between 4.4-7.5%.

Bitter: An English word implying a depth of hop bitterness. The alcohol content is usually around 3.75-4%. If the word Best or Special is also present the alcohol content is slightly higher at 4-4.75%. If the words Extra Special are present this denotes an alcohol content of 5.5%.

Export: In Germany this means a pale bottom-fermented beer with an alcohol content of 5.25-5.5% Outside Germany this indicates a premium beer.

Ice Beer: The beer has been frozen at some stage.

Lager: A bottom-fermented beer.

Lambic: Wheat beer unique to Belgium. Alcohol content 4.4%.

Pilsener/Pilsner/Pils: A term generally applied to any golden coloured, dry, bottom-fermenting beer. A classic Pilsner is characterised by the hoppiness of its flowery aroma and dry finish. Its origins are in the CzechRepublic from the town of Pilsen.
Stout: An extra-dark, top-fermenting brew made from roasted malts.

Trappist: An order of monks with 5 breweries in Belgium and one in the Netherlands. It is illegal to use this term for any other product. Their beers are strong with an alcoholic content of between 6-12%.

Tripel: A Dutch word meaning the strongest beer of the house. These beers are often pale in colour and top fermented.

Weisse/Weissbier, Weizenbier: German for 'white' beer.

Eau, What A Choice!

It's the best thirst quenching drink there is. It's not alcohol but it's a bargain !

Mineral water, (eau minérale) both still (plate) and sparkling (gazeuse) is exceptionally good value for money and substantially cheaper to buy in France. Why this is so is perplexing as unlike alcohol, there is no tax to blame.

There is often a vast selection of different brands at the hypermarkets. Some, such as Evian, Volvic and the comparatively expensive Perrier will be familiar, yet some of the lesser known brands are just as good.
For example in Aldi the sparkling River brand is just 22p for 1.5 litres which we believe to be under half the price of the equivalent in the UK. Also in Aldi is a still water - Lucheux - which at 12.5p a 2 litre bottle must merit some space in your boot.In our blind tasting, we sampled a some mineral waters at fridge temperature. Here are a selection of commonly available mineral waters:

Badoit: Slightly sparkling from the Loire.
Ave Price: FF3.50 (40p) 1L
Comment: Slightly salty
Contrexéville: From Vosges. Reputedly good for the kidneys. Has a slightly diuretic effect.
Ave Price: FF2.9 (33p) 1.5L
Comment: Slightly salty.
Evian: From the town of Evian at Lake Geneva.It has a slightly diuretic effect.
Ave Price: FF4.20 (47p) 2L
Comment: Tasteless but thirst quenching.
Perrier: A very well-marketed mineral water from Nîmes. Full of sparkle and is generally used as soda water in France.
Ave Price: FF4.5 (51p) 1L
Comment: Most refreshing with almost no flavour.
River: Sparkling water
Ave Price: FF1.75 (19p) 1.5L
Comment: Slightly chalky on the palate.
Vichy: A sparkler from Vichy.
Ave Price: FF3 (34p) 1.5L
Comment: Like bicarbonate of soda.
Vittel: A still yet rugged mineral water - from Nancy.
Ave Price: FF2.80 (32p) 1.5L
Comment: Refreshing and slightly sweet.
Volvic: A still water from Auvergne filtered through volcanic rock.
Ave Price: FF3 (34p) 1.5L
Comment: Smooth silky taste.

Tobacco Prices Up In Smoke!

Top up in France . It is cheaper than the UK, and there's no limit for personal use !

Product	Duty Free	France	U.K.
Cigarettes	Av. £	Av. £	Av. £
Benson & Hedges	£1.39	£2.00	£3.28
Camel	£1.49	£2.21	£3.28
Dunhill	£1.70	£2.62	£3.28
Gauloises	£1.20	£2.37	£3.20
Gitanes	£1.85	£1.68	£3.17
John Player Special	£1.49	£1.74	£3.00
Lambert & Butler	£1.39	£2.14	£2.79
Marlboro	£1.53	£2.25	£3.28
Philip Morris	£1.49	£2.22	£3.28
Rothmans	£1.49	£2.07	£3.28
Silk Cut	£1.49	£2.25	£3.28
Superkings	£1.40	£2.13	£3.09
Tobacco			
Drum 50g	£2.20	£2.56	£7.10
Golden Virginia 40g *50g	£3.10*	£2.00	£7.57
Old Holborn 40g *50g	£2.10*	£2.25	£7.57
Samson 50g	£2.10	£2.25	£7.47
Cigars x 5			
King Edward Imperial	£2.99	£4.00	£8.95
Villager Export	£2.10	£3.75	£4.70

The above table illustrates the savings that can be made when buying tobacco Duty Free . If you wish to exceed Duty Free limits, you can top up in France. Tobacco can be purchased from outlets called 'Tabacs'. These shops are similar to our own newsagents. Cigarette and tobacco prices are state regulated in France when sold through a tabac. This is not true of tobacco sold in cafés, bars and petrol stations where prices tend to be higher. Unlike the UK, French supermarkets do not sell tobacco at all. Most tabacs are closed on Sundays and bank holidays. Most accept sterling and credit cards.

The Epicurean's Tour of The Shops

When shopping in any French town what stands out is the variety of traditional gastronomic shops, some of which have no comparable counterpart in the UK. It must be a cultural thing but very simply, the French like to specialise.

Take the Boucherie for example - the butcher. The Boucherie sells all types of meat and poultry - except pork. To buy pork you need to visit the Charcuterie - which means cooked meat.

The Charcuterie, originally a pork butcher, has evolved into a pork based delicatessen. Visiting a Charcuterie for the first time will shift your perception of the humble pig 'le cochon' in gastro-nomic terms forever! Now you will see it as pâté, terrin, rillets, rillons, hams, dried sausages, fresh sausages, pieds de porc, andouillettes boudins noirs et blancs. This pork lovers haven also offers ready made pork meals with a selection of plats de jour that just need heating up when you get home.

Horse meat is also popular in France and this is sold in outlets known as Boucherie Chevaline - horse meat butcher, generally identifiable by a horse's head sign.

Cheese, a much revered commodity in France, is produced with exacting procedures by the highly skilled maître fromager (master cheese specialist). The shop to visit to really get the feel of the cheese culture at its best is the Fromagerie - a specialist cheese shop which will probably have around 300 varieties on sale.

A cross between a grocery store and delicatessen is the Epicerie. The store sells cheese and fresh meat amongst other food products. These days the Epricerie is based a little on the Supermarché and an Alimentation Général - a general store and has lost its authenticity somewhat.

Calais and Boulogne both being fishing towns are awash with fresh seafood. You can buy the catch of the day from the Poissonerie. This could be a fishmonger or just a stall.

Another example of specialisation in action is the Boulangerie - the bakery. The shelves are stacked with all types of unusual bread and buns and occasionally cakes and quiches too.

But for a fiendishly good selection of cakes and biscuits, it is over to the Pâtisserie for specialist cakes, flans and tarts. The Pâtisserie sometimes sells ice-cream too.

Sweets, not the comm-ercial pre-wrapped type, but handmade sweets such as bon-bons, nougat and crystallised fruit, have their own home in a Confiserie or Chocolaterie - a high class sweet or chocolate shop. The products are a little pricey but good quality, delicious and beautifully packaged for you.

For fresh fruit, flowers and vegetables and a myriad of fresh French delights the best place is the Marché - outdoor market. These are generally open on a Saturday or Wednesday.

You could of course, by-pass the specialist shops which offer pleasant insightful echoes of French daily life and culture - a shopping experience unlike any you can have in the UK. You could, instead shop in one of the immense Hypermarché - hypermarkets. The total anonymity that comes with being one of hundreds of trolley pushers walking around thousands of kilometres of floor space in a state of suspended reality is an experience all of its own!

Say Cheese

Take a glass of your favourite wine, break off a little baguette, fill it with your favourite cheese - Voila! a slice of French culture.

The inherent passion for wine within the French culture is closely followed by their love for cheese, so much so that France has become renowned for its remarkably large array of cheeses. Incredibly, the number of different varieties is believed to be in excess of 700. Not only do supermarkets dedicate large areas of floor space to their cheese counters, but the French also have specialist cheese shops.

These quaint shops are called 'Fromageries' (cheese shops) offering cheese in all its colours and consistencies.

Though nasal passages have to grapple with the pungent aroma that hangs heavily in the air, the palate can look forward to a delightful epicurean experience. It is at the fromagerie that the finest cheeses can be found,

thanks to the resident maître fromager (master cheese specialist). His highly skilled job combines the complexities of cheese selection, storage and the delicate process of 'affinage'. This is the art of ageing a young cheese to maturity so that it is offered in its prime.

To the uninitiated though, the cheese counter must look like a daunting display of yellow and white hues with the odd shout of blue. No matter how tempting these colours look, one wonders about the taste. Fortunately, it is customary for supermarkets and fromageries to offer dégustation (sampling) upon request.

Fromageries to try are La Maison du Fromage, 1 rue Andre-Gerschel in Calais. In Boulogne you can try La Cave du Fromager, 23 rue de Lille which is connected to a nearby speciality cheese restaurant called Restaurant des Fromages.

Boulogne is especially favoured with Phillippe Olivier's cheese shop at 43 rue Thiers, reputedly, the most famous cheese vendor in the world. Phillippe Olivier has created a heavenly cave of cheese and a visit there is a must for any cheese lover.

Although not possible to list all available cheeses, some will already be familiar to you, such as Normandy's Camembert and Brie from Ile de France (especially the President label) are widely found and at a third less than UK prices. Fromages fermiers (farmhouse cheese) are considered to be the finest of all cheeses. These are made by small producers using milk from their own farm animals. When unpasteurised milk is used this is denoted with the words 'lait cru'. Other varieties to try are:

Le Brin. A small hexagon shaped cheese. Made from cows' milk, it is mild and creamy. The edible rind has a delicate, pleasant aroma. The special method of production leaves the cheese high in calcium and phosphorus.

Cantorel Roquefort. A speciality of South-West France, this blue cheese is ripened in the caves of Cambalou for at least 90 days in accordance with its Appellation d'Origine Contrôlée. Made entirely from sheep's milk, its distinctive taste is best enjoyed with Barsac or Sauternes wines.

Chimay. You may already be familiar with the Belgian Trappist beer of this name. Chimay is also a range of six Belgian Trappist cheeses. Chimay Bière is flavoured with Chimay beer and is a treat for the palate.

Rambol. Decorated with walnuts it looks like a small gateau.It is smooth with a mellow flavour.

Société Roquefort. Creamy in texture and distinguished by its marbled green and ivory colouring.

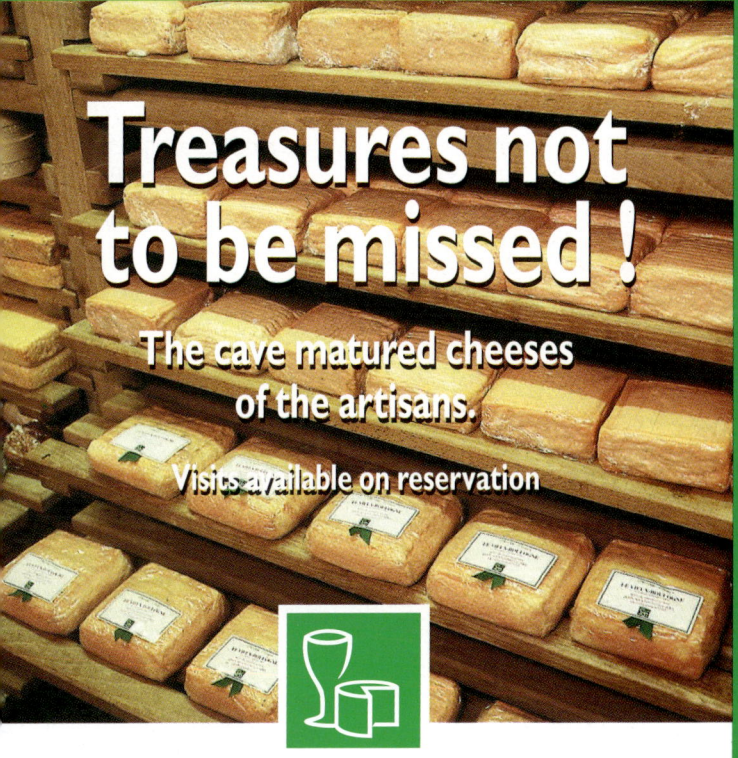

St. Agur. A creamy blue veined cheese from the Auvergne. It has a mild flavour and sits well on a cheese board.

Tartare. A cream cheese spread from Périgord made with garlic and herbs. It comes as a full fat cheese and for slimmers there's **Tartare Light** with just a third of the calorie content.

Trappe de Belval. Made by nuns at the abbey of Belval located near to Hesdin. It has a rather hard exterior covering concealing a creamy and mild interior.

Serving suggestions:

•Cheese is at its best served at room temperature, remove from the fridge at least one hour before required.
•Allow 2oz per person for a cheese board and 4oz per person for a cheese and wine evening.
•Select 3-4 different types of cheese for an attractive display, especially on a cheese board.

Storage Tips:

Fortunately, most hard cheeses are freezable as long as they are not overmature when frozen. This is not recommended for soft cheeses.

Generally, the following guidelines for fridge storage apply:

•Fresh Cheese (soft cheese) Eat within a few days.
•Blue Cheese Can be kept up to 3 weeks.
•Goats', Ewe's Milk Cheese will keep for up to two weeks.
•Always store cheese in the lowest part of the fridge wrapped in foil or in an air proof container to prevent drying out.

Fromagerie

French Bread

It's the law! Every French village must have its own boulangerie (bakery) supplying the villagers with freshly baked bread every day of the week.

Governed by French law, the boulangerie emerges as the single most important shop in any village, faithfully providing the villagers with an essential part of their staple diet - bread.

As with all things French an etiquette has evolved around bread. It is generally considered unacceptable to serve bread purchased in the morning in the evening. No self respecting Frenchman would dare to insult his guests in this way. However, left over bread may be used perhaps for dunking into hot chocolate - in specially formulated wide cups - or alternatively can be cooked in soup.

The most famous and popular French bread (both within and outside France) is the long, thin baguette or French stick. It has a uniform length; and its weight - governed by French law - must be 250 grams!

Although the baguette is made simply from soft flour, yeast, water and a pinch or two of salt, it has an appealing fluffy texture and can be enjoyed just as well on its own as it can with food. However, its short life span means that it must be consumed soon after it has been baked. Bakeries routinely bake bread twice a day to ensure fresh bread for a very discriminating public.

Other extreme variations on the baguette are the ficelle (a word which literally means string). It is the thinnest loaf available. In contrast un pain or Pariesen is double the size of a baguette. Some compromise is reached with petit pains and the bâtons which are much shorter than the baguette and similar to large rolls. For breakfast (le petit dèjeuner) the French will also enjoy a Continental breakfast (better known in France as viennoisie). This includes such delicious treats as the famous pastry style croissant. This familiar crescent shaped roll was Marie Antoinett's inadvertent contribution to the Western breakfast culture. She introduced them to the Parisian Royals in the late 18th century where they proved to be an epicurean hit. In Marie Antoinette's home country of Vienna, however, the croissant had been making a regular appearance at the breakfast table as early as 1683. It was in this year that the Polish army saved the city from Turkish hands and in celebration the Viennese baked a crescent shaped creation based on the Ottoman flag - voila, the croissant was born!

The croissant is similar to puff pastry - made with yeast dough and butter and is usually accompanied by some confit (crystallized fruit) or confiture (various flavours of jam). Sometimes it is served with jam, cheese or chocolate and can be savoured hot or cold. Traditionally, the croissant is dunked by the French into their coffee in specially made wide cups designed for this purpose. This French idiosyncrasy can also be traced back to the late 17th century. The defeated Turks had left some sacks of coffee beans before they left Vienna. These were discovered by a group of Armenian Jews who started the croissant dunking tradition.

There are also many other tempting and unusual styles of bread available at the specialist boulangerie (bakery) or the boulangerie counter of the hypermarket.

French Bread

Here are some suggestions you may like to try:

Pain au chocolat - a croissant style bun imbued with chocolate (delicious when warm).

Brioche. a breakfast bun made from yeast, dough, eggs and butter, giving it a wonderful sweet, buttery aroma and taste.

Couronnes. A baguette style bread in the shape of a ring.

Pain aux noix. An outstanding bread baked with walnuts on the inside and on the crust.

Pain aux olives. A delicious bread with olives and olive oil.

Pain de sègle. Made with rye and wheat.

Pain noir. Wholemeal bread.

Pain de son. Wholemeal bread fortified with bran.

Pain de mie. Sliced bread with a soft crust. Used for sandwiches.

Pain biologique. This bread is baked with organic wholemeal flour.

Pain campagne. Flatter than baguettes but also heavier. They have the advantage of staying fresh for longer.

Pain au Levain/Pain à l'ancienne. Both these names refer to French bread made from sour dough. This is probably one of the oldest styles of French bread there is.

In Calais you can visit Fred at Bd Jacquard situated near the Town Hall (map ref: D4)

In Boulogne try Joly Desenclos, at 44-46 rue de Lille (vieille ville map ref: F5). Both these boulangeries have tea rooms.

Specialities at the Pâtisserie

If, like the French, you have a sweet tooth then a visit to a Pâtisserie gives a whole new meaning to the phrase 'Let Them Eat Cake'.

In true French style, even the last course of a meal is not the least. Dinner in any French home will always conclude with a sweet, which if not home made will be bought from the Pâtisserie - a specialist cake shop. The Pâtisserie may also have a selection of handmade confectionary.

Like French wines and cheese, different areas of France have their own regional indulgences on offer. For instance, from Provence comes Marrons Glacés and Fruits Glacés: the former is an autumnal treat of chestnuts in vanilla-flavoured syrup; the latter is fresh fruit in sugar syrup.

Normandy, famous for its apple orchards, offers Tarte Normande. A variation is Gratin de Pommes Vallée D'Auge - it is no ordinary apple crumble; it is soaked in Calvados (an apple brandy produced in Normandy) and then baked in crème fraîche. The Pas de Calais too has an indigenous tart whose thick pastry has led to the name Tarte au Gros Bord. It is adorned simply with custard and sugar.

Other offerings include:
Gaufres a La Flamande - waffles powdered with sugar and sometimes served with whipped cream.

Tarte au Fromage - Cheese cake made from eggs and cottage cheese.

Nougat Glacé - From Provence a frozen honey and almond desert.

Pastis Gascon - Thin pastry, layered between the folds with vanilla sugar and butter, adorned with apple and marinated in Armagnac.

Baba au Rhum - A yeast product soaked in rum flavoured syrup. Best eaten with a spoon.

Other Shopping Ideas

**With the pound so strong, shopping in France is altogether cheaper these days.
Here are some tips and shopping ideas.**

TIP:
Serious bargain hunters should time their trip to France with the French sales. These happen twice a year - in January and in August and generally last between one to two months. You can pick up some fantastic bargains!

TIP:
Also in August is the Braderie. This is like a giant car boot sale all over the town.

TIP:
Take a cooler bag with you just in case you want to buy fresh products such as cheese or fish. Your purchases will stay fresher for longer and you will avoid any pungent smells on the journey home.

Tip:
Timing is essential. Shops close at lunch time.

Jam (Confiture)
There is a vast selection of confiture. In particular, the brand 'Bonne Maman' which is widely available in the UK can be found for a third to half the price in the main hypermarkets and supermarkets, including Tesco.

Cous Cous
Lovers of cous cous will be pleased to know that you can buy it at half the UK price. Carrefour was the cheapest outlet for this commodity at FF4.95 (62p) for a 1kg pack with other supermarkets close behind. In the UK cous cous is usually sold in half kilo packs at the same price!

Anchovies
You get a wider selection of anchovies, and at half price in France- good value at the hypermarkets.

Other Shopping Ideas

Cider (Cidre)

On French supermarket shelves, and in some cash & carries, both French and UK ciders are on sale. There are differences, notably that French cider tends to contain less alcohol, around 2.4% as opposed to 5%+ for the British ciders. British ciders such as Strongbow and Bulmers are generally available in France at about half the UK price.

Coke and Pepsi

Whether you are buying cans or bottles, these are at least 25% cheaper in France. Eastenders is selling Coke at 21p a can and Pepsi Max at 18p.

Pasta

Certain brands of pasta such as Isabella and Monte Regal in supermarkets represent very good value for money. For instance all shapes of Isabella pasta costs around 52p per kilo compared to a similar pasta in the UK costing 95p.

Mustard (Moutard)

Not only is mustard substantially cheaper in France, but there is also a much wider selection. For the sake of price comparison, we will use Dijon mustard which is widely available in both countries. Prices start at FF1.75 (22p) for 370g jar of Dijon mustard compared to a typical UK price of 59p for 250g.

English mustard is slightly hotter than Dijon mustard. Try 'seeded' Dijon mustard; it has a particularly delicate flavour.

Filtered Coffee - (Café Moulu)

Fans of filtered coffee will be pleased to know that this product is available widely and at half the UK prices. Try the taste of even the cheapest brands of filtered coffee and you will not be disappointed. A 1kg (4 x 250g pack) can be found for as little as FF29.00. Try Arabica.

Other Shopping Ideas

Chocolate Milkshake Drinks

The Nestlé Nesquick drinks are normally substantially cheaper in all French supermarkets - typically around £2.47 for 1 kilo. In the UK the standard 225gm Nesquick drink retails for around £1 (equivalent to £4 per kilo).This represents a 40% saving on the UK supermarket price.

Other French chocolate drinks worth trying are Schovit 800g (in Aldi) and Goucao/Opticao 800g (at most supermarkets) which cost around FF9.45 and FF10.85 respectively. Not only do the prices compare favourably but they are also very tasty and a hit with the kids.

Fruit Juice (Jus de Fruit)

Generally, fruit juice is almost a third less in France. This is especially true of brands such as Recre, Goldhorn and Lagona ranging from 29p-43p per 1 litre carton.

In the UK the price range would be 59p-89p.

In Aldi, rue Mollien we came across 20cl carton orange drinks which are ideal for lunch boxes at the amazing price of 9p per carton! The name of this product is Orangen and can be purchased in packs of 10 for FF7.45 (90p) - under half the price of the nearest UK equivalent.

Crisps (Les Chips)

Crisps are known as 'Les Chips' in France and are generally of a reasonable quality. The big packs are very economical.

In particular Aldi stocks ready salted, paprika and bolognaise flavoured crisps in 200g packets (equivalent to 10 small packets in the UK) for under FF3 (32p).

From all the crisps sampled, these were the least greasy, and the tastiest - ideal for your parties.

Other Shopping Ideas

Peanuts (Cacahuètes)
Look out for peanuts - 30% cheaper than the UK price!

Olives
In general olives (both black and green) are about 30% cheaper in the French supermarkets. In Aldi try the Olives Vertes Beldi which we found very tasty. Other hypermarkets also have a tasty range of olives. They are great in a baguette with camembert and make a filling snack.

Olive Oil (Huile d'olives)
The finest French olive oils - like French wines - come from named origins and even Appellations Controllées. They have a gentle flavour tempered with slight sweetness and are great as condiments, but not suitable for cooking.

These olive oils have low acidity (sometimes as little as 0.2%) which is significant because acidity affects the rate at which the oil deteriorates. Labels of assured finest quality to look out for are 'Huile de Provence' and 'Huile d'Olives Nyons' (the latter is subject to quality control with its own Appellation d'Origine. This sort of quality is expensive and could be up to £30.00 in the UK (less in France). Generally, you are likely to purchase brands that are commercially blended.

Look for either Extra Virgin (Vierge) or First Cold Pressing (Premier Presson Froid) whose acidity is never more than 1%, but is better still at 0.5%, Fine Virgin olive oil at 1.5% or less, and Ordinary Virgin olive oil whose acidity level is 3%. This sort of quality olive oil in the UK is rarely below £6.00 per litre yet in France the price is around FF28.00 (£3.50).

Rice (Riz)
Long grain rice can be found for under FF5 (53p) per kilo in French supermarkets. Comparable rice in the UK is around 99p.

Other Shopping Ideas

Fish (Poisson)

Being fishing ports, both Calais and Boulogne are rich with fish restaurants.

If you have enjoyed a fish or seafood meal, you may be inclined to buy your own to take home. The hypermarkets have comprehensive fish and seafood sections or better still, you can visit a fish monger *(poissonnerie)*. There is also a fish market in Boulogne port selling freshly caught sea food. Generally prices are around 10% cheaper but prices vary in accordance with the catch and the season.

SPECIAL OFFER:

In Calais, you can visit: Les Délices de la Mer at 160 bd Lafayette. Monsieur Blondel, the owner is offering readers of The Channel Hopper's Guide a **FREE KIPPER** with every purchase - but don't forget to show your copy of the guide.

Poissonnerie

Other Shopping Ideas

Mountain Bikes (VTT)

Although we are unable to give a true comparison on mountain bikes, we can say that the hypermarkets do have good value bikes. Adult mountain bikes start at under £100 and children's mountain bikes can be found for around £40. It is difficult to find these prices in the UK.

Floor Tiles

Situated next door to most hypermarket complexes is a DIY shop called 'Leroy Merlin' specialising in DIY products. DIY enthusiasts will be pleased to know that the average price of floor and wall tiles can be up to half the UK price. Particularly good value were Terracotta floor tiles at just over £5.00 per square metre. Terracotta Pots (Terre Cuite). These are sold at Leroy Merlin and the hypermarket at vastly cheaper prices than in the UK. For instance a window box of 50x 17cm is around FF24.95 (£3.10) in Continent and £12.99 in the UK.

Glassware

Duralex, Luminarc and Cristal D'Arques are names you may already be familiar with. They are available at the hypermarkets at prices that are at least 20% less than in the UK! You can visit **Cristal d'Arques** factory at Zone Industrielle, RN43 Arques 62510, Tel: 00 33 321 93 46 96 (A26 motorway, Arques exit). There is a museum and a visitor centre where you can make purchases. Prices are generally about 20% less than the French retail outlets, but you have to call in advance. Cost of the visit is FF30.00 and includes a gift. Under sixteens are not admitted.

Lace (Dentelles)

One of the local industries of Calais is Lace making. The French take their lace so seriously that there is a museum in Calais to display it. Purchasing lace in France is not always cheaper, but you do get a wider choice. Look out for the specialist lace shops called dentellières.

Other Shopping Ideas

Garden Furniture (Jardinage)

Garden furniture is often half the UK price of the equivalent and tempting to buy - but you will need a lot of space in your car! At Leroy Merlin (next to Auchan), Continent, Carrefour and Auchan, there is a good selection of both plastic and pine table and chair sets. Plastic chairs start from FF19.95 (£2.50) and plastic tables 85cm in diameter from as little as FF119.00 (£14.90). A pine table and chair set can be found for only FF599.00 (£75.00).

Garden parasols are also around £10.00 cheaper in France.

Tissues

Both boxed and handbag size are at least 25% cheaper across the board.

Loo Rolls

Around half price in the hypermarkets.

Batteries

Around 20% cheaper in the hypermarkets.

Light Bulbs

Not a huge saving to be made, but 15% is enough to bring a little light.

Pots & Pans

You may already be familiar with the names 'Le Creuset' and 'Tefal'. These two popular quality brands of pots and pans are both manufactured in France. You can purchase these in the French hypermarkets and supermarkets for as little as half the UK price. For example, the Le Creuset 20cm saucepan is typically sold in the UK for around £33.00 yet it is available at French hypermarkets at around FF127 (£15.50).

Razor Blades

A set of five blades is over £1.00 cheaper across the range available. Apparently, more than just a shaving off the price.

Washing Powder

Ariel washing powder is substantially cheaper in France. Are they cleaning up in the UK?

Other Shopping Ideas

Pushchairs & Prams

We have received a number of letters about pushchairs and prams. Apparently these are cheaper in the hypermarkets. We have not yet substantiated these claims. If you do plsease let us know.

Computer Games

A visit to Toys R Us in Cité Europe or indeed any hypermarket may pay dividends. Computer games are at around a third cheaper. For instance Mario Kart game costs FF399, £44.33 in France, in the UK it costs £59.99.

Children's Clothes

A tip reluctantly divulged from a discerning shopper

Tip:

'I always make a bee-line for Leclerc supermarkets in particular since they stock Galipette - considered in the UK to be a designer label, with trousers (for example) selling for around £35-£40 in children's cloths boutiques. These clothes are up to a third of the price in Leclerc. This supermarket also stocks several bargain clothing ranges including KidOkay, which have undeniable French styling and are very reasonably priced.

If travelling further afield especially to Paris, pack an empty suitcase and stock up at Du Pareil Au Mem, a star in the clothing fermament - where an entire season's wardrobe; sweaters, trousers, dresses, coats, accessories, PJs and so on will set you back around £50. It's definitely worth looking out for this label.

Now I have just given away my greatest secret and everyone will be rushing over to France to clothe their children in style'.
Tracy Posner, Ealing.

PS.
Leclerc supermarket has a reputation for value-for-money, economy lines. There is a branch in Boulogne off the N142 road along the river Liane, signposted Le Touquet. Refer to its entry in earlier pages.

Eating Out

Everything stops for lunch in France. Take time out to enjoy a pastime the French take very seriously - eating!

You know lunchtime has arrived in France when you see the sign **'fermé'** (closed) on shop doors. As the shops and factories close, the restaurants open for business, offering a choice of cuisine and ambience.

Choosing a restaurant is easy as they generally display their menus outside. Steer clear of empty restaurants - in our experience, they generally deserve to be so!

If you have booked a table be sure to be on time, as your table is unlikely to be saved for more than ten minutes, especially on Sundays, when everyone likes to eat out 'en famille'.

Most restaurants cater for the tourists by offering a menu touristique usually written in English or with an English translation, alongside the regional dishes. This is usually good value for money and comprises such dishes as steak and French fries.

One item that will be missing from any French menu is the traditional two-slices-of-bread British sandwich. You may find it referred to on the menu at cafés or brasseries, but it will never be served in sliced bread. The most popular 'sandwich' is the croque monsieur which is basically ham and cheese in a ficelle (a slimmer version of a baguette). There is also a feminine version of this known as croque-madame which comes with a fried egg too.

Alternatively, you could choose the Prix Fixé menu, a set price menu which may include the plat du jour (dish of the day) or spécialité de la maison (house special). These are a better choice for those wishing to try a more local dish, usually seafood or frogs legs - cuisses de grenouilles. For extra choice you could experiment with the à la carte menu or indulge in the menu gastronomique for finer quality food.

Not all prices will be highlighted on the menu. The letters SG may sit alongside some dishes and stand for selon grosseur (according to weight). This applies to dishes that, for practical purposes, are sold by weight, such as lobster or fish. In this instance it is advisable to find out the price before you order.

If the words service compris (service included) or service et taxes compris (service and taxes included) are on the menu, that means the prices include a service charge. However, odd coins are usually left for the waiter. Otherwise, it is customary to leave a tip of around 10%.

Meals are never rushed in restaurants even if you only want a snack and a drink at one of the cafés. You can while away the time at your leisure and this isacceptable. However if your are eating to a deadline, pay for your meal when it arrives, as catching the waiter's eye later may prove a challenge.

Tip:
Go for French food while in France. This not only adds to the French experience, but also makes good economic sense; traditional British food and drink such as tea, Scotch whisky and gin or a plate of bacon and eggs are expensive. So check out the menu or 'tarif des consommations' (if in a café or bar) for something that tickles your palate and accompany it with wine (vin ordinaire) or draught beer (pression).

Alternatively French spirits and soft drinks are generally inexpensive relative to their British counterparts on the menu.

Tip: To get the attention of the waiter lift your index finger and call Monsieur - not garçon. A waitress should be addressed as Madam or Madmoiselle.

Tip:
When ordering coffee, be specific and say exactly what you would like. Unlike British restaurants, just ordering a coffee will not do. The exception to this is during the breakfast meal when coffee is served in large wide-mouthed coffee cups - specially designed for dunking - and milk is a standard accompaniment.

Coffee Styles.

Un café, s'il vous plaît
You will receive an espresso coffee, strong and black in a small espresso cup

Un café au lait s'il vous plaît
You will receive an espresso coffee with milk on the side.

Une crème s'il vous plaît
You will receive a small white coffee

Une crème grande s'il vous plaît
You will receive a white coffee served in normal size cup.

Terms on a French Menu

Les Viandes	Meat
L'agneau	Lamb
Assiette Anglaise	Plate of cold meat
Bifteck haché	Hamburger
Contrefilet	Sirloin
Entrecôte	Steak
Foie	Liver
Foie gras	Goose liver
Faux filet	Sirloin Steak
Jambon	Ham
Langue	Tongue
Rognons	Kidneys
Les Poissons	Fish
Anchois	Anchovy
Anguille	Eel
L'Assiette de fruits de mer	Sea food platter
L'Assiette Nordique	Smoked fish platter
Crevette grise	Shrimp
Crevette rose	Prawn
Fruit de mer	Shellfish
Gamba	Large prawn
Homard	Lobster
Huître	Oyster
Limand	Lemon sole
Saumon	Salmon
Thon	Tuna
Truite	Trout
Truite arc en ciel	Rainbow trout

Volaille	Poultry
Canard	Duck
Dindon	Turkey
Oie	Goose
Faisan	Pheasant
Perdreau	Partridge
Pigeon	Pigeon
Poulet	Chicken(roast)
Poularde	Chicken (boiled)
Poussin	Spring chicken
Sauce	Sauce
Béarnaise	Sauce from egg yolks, shallots, wine & tarragon
Béchamel	White sauce with herbs
Beurre blanc	Loire sauce with butter, wine and shallots
Beurre noir	Blackened butter
Meunière	Butter & lemon sauce
Miscellaneous	
Braisé	Braised
Brochette	Skewer
Brouillade	Stew with oil
Brouillé	Scrambled
Fumé	Smoked
Gratinée	Grill browned
Grillé	Grilled
Suprème	Chicken breast or game bird
Terrine	Coarse paté

RESTAURANTS

The following restaurants are some suggested places to eat. Remember that unless the restaurant advertises that it is a 'non-stop' establsihment lunch time meals are strictly served between 12pm-3pm.

CALAIS

Aquar'aile
255 rue Jean Moulin
Plage de Calais
On the 4th floor of a block of seafront flats.
Fine seafood restaurant
Per head: FF90-FF230
Special offer: On presentation of your guide, a brandy or a tipple to round off the meal.

La Braserade
8 Rue Jean de Vienne
Calais
Carvery style & menu
Per head: FF98-170

Cafe de Champagne
46 rue de la Mer
Calais
Pizza, steak, eggs, and loud music
Per head: FF25-60

Le Détroit
5 Boulevard de la Résistance
Calais
Fish, seafood, woodfire grills
Per head: From FF100

Les Dunes
Part of an hotel
48 Route National
Bleriot Plage
Junction 14 off A16 motorway
Calais
Seafood
Per head: From FF100

La Goulu
26 rue de la Mer
Calais
Grills - steaks
Per head: From FF80

Au Coq d'Or
31 Place d'Armes
62100 Calais
French Cuisine
Per head: From FF59
Special offer: One kir offered on presentation of your guide.

Le Blanc Nez
Sangatte. Junction 12 off A16 motorway
French cuisine
Per head: From FF79
Special offer: One free aperitif on presentation of this guide.

Le Channel
3 Boulevard de la Resistance
Sweetbreads and fish
Per head: various fixed priced menus

Lunch on a Mountain Top

Enjoy wonderful French cuisine in this family run restaurant. Situated on top of Mont d'Hubert at Escalles it has exceptional panoramic views *- on a clear day you can even see England.*

OPEN DAILY
Set menus from
FF78 (£8.50)

A **free** bottle of French wine per table for Channel Hopper's readers on production of this Guide.

Offer cannot be used in conjunction with any other offer

FREE WINE for CHANNEL HOPPERS!

LE THOME DE GAMOND
Mont Hubert, 62179 Escalles
Tel: 00 333 21 82 32 03
Fax: 00 333 21 82 32 61

How To Get There
Take the D940 from the Blériot-Plage in Calais centre following the sign 'Boulogne par la corniche'. Follow the D940 road for around 15 minutes. It is situated on the left. From the A16 motorway exit at junction (sortie) 12.

La Manche — SANGATTE — BLÉRIOT-PLAGE — CALAIS
Cap Blanc Nez
ESCALLES — Frethun Terminal
Cap Gris Nez — WISSANT — AUDINGHEN — sortie Cap Blanc Nez
AMBLETEUSE
MARQUISE
WIMEREUX
BOULOGNE

Le Thomé de Gamond
Musée Transmanche
(A16 SORTIE N°12)

Open daily from noon to 3pm.
Open evenings in July & August from 6.30pm to 9.00pm.
Groups catered for (from 10 220 people).

Histoire Ancienne
20 rue royale
Calais
Greek specialities, grills
and fish

Le Milano
14 Place d'Armes
Calais
The only pizzeria in
Calais
Per head: FF75
Special Offer: On
presentation of this guide
a free glass of white wine
with your meal.

Le Grand Bleu
8 rue Jean-Pierre Avron
Bassin de la Colonne
(opp. Calais port), Calais
Fish, seafood
Per head: FF100

Le Saint-Charles
47 Place d'Armes (north
side, Calais
Fish - monkfish in cider,
scallops and sirloin
Per head: FF65 - FF185

Le Sole Meunière
1 Boulevard de la
Resistance
Swish fish fishes and
steak grills
Per head: From FF100

**Four excellent
restaurants
on the D940**

Le Thomé de Gamond
Mont Hubert
Escalles
Seafood
Per head: From FF100
Special offer: One bottle
of wine to take home
after the meal on
presentation of this
guide.

L'Epicure
1 rue de la Gare
Wimereux
Seafood
Per head: From FF125

Le Relais de la Brocante
2 rue de Ledinghem
Wimille
Situated in the village
close to the church.
Original ideas -
kippertoast flavoured with
coffee beans & tripe
sausage with juniper.
Per Head: From FF80

Restaurant du Cap
Place de la Mairie
Escalles, Cap Blanc-Nez
Seafood
Per head: FF89

Looking for real French Cuisine?

Just 10 minutes from the Terminal,
Daniel and François Vinck, owner of

LE BLANC NEZ

Restaurant

welcome you to enjoy typical
French cuisine at affordable prices
Menus at 89F, 119F, 149F, 179F

119FF Menu

Salmon and sea scallops pate
Season soup
Home made pate
Home made goat cheese pate with
sweet pepper
Six snails of burgondy
Mussels in white wine
Smoked salmon with toast

Skate fish with parsley sauce
Fisher's pepper steak (fish)
Salmon with pear and roquefort sauce
Duck with peach cream sauce
Pepper steak
Grilled lamb chop

Cheeses or sweet

Menus can change with seasons.

Seafood and
A la Carte specialities
Fine Wine List
Open all day - closed Sunday
evening and all day Monday

Special Offer:
A **Free** aperitif of your choice
with your meal on
presentation of this guide.

Restaurant
LE BLANC NEZ

at Sangatte
(on the main road past the church.
Tel: 00 33 321 88 00 53
Fax: 00 33 321 77 64

How to Get There:
Leave le Shuttle and follow signs for
Boulogne (A16). Leave A16 at
junction 12 and follow signs to
Sangatte. Turn left at the end of the
road. We are on the left

BOULOGNE

Le Pot d'Etain
24 Rue du Pot d'Etain
Boulogne
French cuisine
Per head: From FF51

Chez Jules
8 place Dalton
Boulogne
Seafood
Per head: From FF100

Marie-Renée Frémont
28 rue de Lille
Haute Ville, Boulogne
Specialises in cheese
dishes.
Per head: From FF70

Christophe et Laurence
10 rue Coquelin
Boulogne
Deli, steak, brasserie
Per head: FF75

Le Doyen
1 Rue do Doyen
Boulogne
French with emphasis on
fish dishes, candle-lit
Per head: From FF90

La Houblonnière
8 rue Monsigny
Boulogne
Brasserie style
Per head: From FF65

L'Huitrière
11 Place Lorraine
Boulogne
Situated on a
pedestrianised square.
Tiny fish restaurant and
oyster bar
Per head: FF80 & FF120

L'Union de la Marine
18 Bd Gambetta
Boulogne
Seafood
Per head: From FF65

Restaurant de la Pierre
Chaude
19 rue de Lille
Generally French.
Guests can cook their
own meats on heated
boulders
Per head: FF75-125

Sucre-Sale
rue Monsigny off rue
Thiers
Good for salads,
savouries and sweets
Per head: Various

Le Matelote
80 Boulevard Sainte-
Beuve, Boulogne
Opposite Nausicaa.
Run by one of France's
leading Chefs

Hotels

Check Out the Automatic Check-Inns

If you are looking to stay overnight or longer, look no further than one of France's best kept secrets. In recent years several chains of budget hotels have been set up on an unmanned auto-check-in basis. Entrance is by credit card through a 'hole in the wall' using the language of your choice, and you can gain access all day and night. The rooms are clean and modern and usually comprise one double and one single bed (bunk style) plus a colour TV with UK channels. A Continental style self-service breakfast is available and usually costs around £2.50 extra per person.

The Formule 1 hotel is exceptionally good value at around £18 per night for up to 3 people. Incredibly, the tariffs in France are based on the room per night and not - as in the UK - per person. Unfortunately there is no en-suite bathroom and the only shower and toilet is a communal one located along the hallway. Mister Bed, is a slightly more expensive hotel in a similar style but it does include an en-suite shower room. These type of hotels are popular so book in advance.

CALAIS
Formula 1 Hotel
Ave Charles de Gaulle
Chemin de Bernieulles
62231 Coquelles Tel:
(00 33) (0) 3 21 826 700
Near to Auchan
Hypermarket. Situated
2km from Eurotunnel.
From the ferry port
take A26, Autoroute
A16, direction
Boulogne, exit
Junction 12 (sortie 12)
Coquelles. Approx. 10
minutes drive.

BOULOGNE
Formula 1 Hotel
Z.I. de l'Inquétrie
Rue Pierre Martin
St Martin Les
Boulogne Tel:
(00 33) (0) 3 21 31 26 28
Opposite Auchan
Hypermarket. From
Calais and Boulogne
take N1 to St. Omer
A26, exit (sortie) ZI
Inquétrie. From St
Omer, A26 to
Boulogne, exit (sortie)
ZI Inquétrie.

ST OMER
Mister Bed Hotel
ZAC du Lobel - N43,
62510 Arques Tel:
(00 33) (0) 3 21 93 81 20
Near the Crystal
D'Arques factory.
From Calais take A26,
exit 3 to St Omer onto
N42 then follow signs
to Arques- Lille via the
Rocade. At the
roundabout with N43
(Arques-Béthune),
follow sign to Arques.

Of course there are a multitude of hotels all over Calais and Boulogne with varying degrees of luxury and facilities.

One hotel that stands out is Le Copthorn Hotel in the village of Coquelles in Calais. A three star hotel of modern design with all the trimmings of a four star hotel - short of a porter. Madame Ganier explained her resistence to upgrading 'we are happy with our tariffs, if we upgrade we will be obliged to increase them'.

Sound reasoning, and why this hotel represents such good value at around £58.00 per room per night for two people.

Copthorne have an in-house health club called 'Cap Forme' which the locals use for a membership fee. However, all guests are welcome to use the swimming pool, gym, solarium, sauna and use the ricochet court (this two player game is similar to squash) at no extra cost. You can also eat at Le Copthorne's Le Vieux Moulin. The cuisine is a mix of local French and international dishes, and the Bar Coquelles offer a relaxing atmosphere to enjoy a drink.

Another highly recommended hotel is the Hôtel Cléry, a delightful country-house hotel located around 9km - 10 minute drive - south of Calais. Owned by Didier and Catherine Legros, two people passionate about their hotel who have created hotel within a most beautiful environment at reasonable rates - from around £37 per room for two people per night.

Other hotels of beauty are Château Cocove, and Château Tilques. Both hotels are in beautiful grounds and make a perfect weekend retreat.

Le Copthorne Hotel

Le Copthorne Hotel Coquelles-Calais
Avenue Charles de Gaulle
62231 Coquelles
Tel: (00 33) (0)3 21 46 60 60 Fax: (00 33) (0)3 21 85 7676

Dine at Le Vieux Moulin and enjoy both

All guests can enjoy the health club at no extra cost

local French dishes and international cuisine

The spacious en-suite rooms are complete with a TV coffee/tea facilities and a trouser press.

SPECIAL OFFER
10% Off
the room price on presentation of *The Channel Hopper's Guide* upon arrival

Set in peaceful woodland near Coquelles, this elegant hotel is only 3 minutes from the Channel Tunnel, 10 minutes from the ferry terminal and 5 minutes from the A26 and A16 motorways.

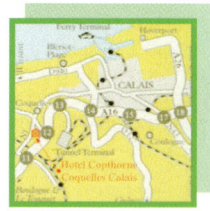

Hotel Cléry

Hotel Cléry***
Château d'Hesdin l'Abbé,
rue du Château 62360 Hesdin l'Abbé
Tel: (00 33) 321 83 19 83 Fax: (00 33) 321 87 52 59

We would like to offer you more than just a bed to sleep in. And during your stay with us, if you feel a spirit of serenity, the sense of well being and contentment, then we have certainly earned the title of a "Hotel de Charme".

22 rooms fully renovated in 1997, from 330FF/room. A restaurant for guests Monday through Friday night.

It is our work, our passion, and above all, our pleasure.
Catherine and Didier Legros

20 minutes from Le Shuttle

10 minutes from Boulogne & Hardelot

20 minutes from Le Touquet

1Km from motorway A16 (take exit 28)

and RN1 direction of Montreuil.

SPECIAL OFFER
A bottle of wine to take home, on presentation of
The Channel Hopper's Guide

Hôtel Château Tilques
Rue du Château
62500 Tilques
Situated on N42, 10kms
before St Omer
Tel: 00 33 (0) 3 21 88 99 99

Le Château de Cocove
62890 Recques-sur-Hem
On D217, 20kms from
Calais
Tel: 00 33 (0) 3 21 82 68 29

Holiday Inn Garden Court
Boulevard des Alliés
62100 Calais
See their advertisement
Tel: 00 33 (0) 3 21 34 69 69

Hôtel Cléry
Rue deu Château
62360 Hesdin l'Abbé
RN1 motorway Boulogne-
Montreuil
Tel: 00 33 (0) 3 21 83 19 93

Les Dunes Hotel
48 Route Nationale
62231 Blériot Plage, Calais
Tel: 00 33 (0) 3 21 34 54 30

Hôtel Faidherbe
12 rue du Château
Boulogne
Tel: 00 33 (0) 3 21 31 60 93

Ibis Plage
170 Bd Ste-Beuve
Boulogne
Tel: 00 33 (0) 3 21 30 12 40

Metropole
51 rue Thiers
Boulogne
Tel: 00 33 (0) 3 21 54 30

Sportifs
rue Faidherbe
Boulogne
Tel: 00 33 (0) 3 21 84 07

How Do You Say?

Pleasantries

Nice to meet you	Enchanté
Yes/No	Oui/non
Good Morning/Good Day	Bonjour
How are you?	Ça va
Good Evening/Good Night	Bonsoir/bonne nuit
Good Bye	Au revoir
See you tommorrow/soon	À demain/bientôt
I've go to go now	Il faut que je me sauve
Excuse me	Excusez-moi
Thank you	Merci
You're welcome	Je vous en prie

Being Understood

I don't speak French	Je ne parle pas français
I don't understand	Je ne comprends pas
Do you speak English?	Parlez-vous anglais?
I don't know how to say it in French	Je ne sais pas le dire en français

Eating Out

A table for two please	Une table pour deux, s'il vous plaît
The menu please	Le menu, s'il vous plaît
Do you have a children's menu?	Avez-vous un menu pour les enfants?
We'll take the set menu, please	Nous prendrons le menu, s'il vous plaît

We would like a dessert	Nous aimerions du dessert
The bill please	L'addition, s'il vous plaît
Is service included?	Le service est compris?
Do you accept credit cards?	Acceptez-vous les cartes de crédit?

Hotels

I'd like a single/double room	Je voudrais une chambre pour une personne/deux personnes
I reserved a room in the name of..	J'ai réservé un chambre au nom de.
I confirmed my booking by phone/letter	J'ai confirmé ma réservation par letter téléphone/lettre
My key, please	Ma clé, s'il vous plaît
I shall be leaving tomorrow	Je partirai demain
What time is breakfast/dinner	Le petit déjeuner/Le dîner est à quelle heure?

How Do You Say?

Directions

How do you get to ......? — Comment fait on pour aller à ...?

How long will it take to get there? — Ça prend combien de temps pour y aller

Where is the nearest supermarket/newsagent/deli? — Où est le supermarché/le tabac/la boulangerie le/la plus près?

Can you tell me how to get to the hotel? — Pouvez-vous me dire fait pour aller à l'hôtel

Where are the toilets? — Où sont les toilettes?

Where's the nearest post box? — Où est la plus proche boîte à lettres?

Where's the nearest phone box? — Où se trouve la cabine téléphonique la plus proche?

Is this the right bus for ...? — C'est bien l'autobus pour... ?

Paying

How much is it? — Ça coûte Combien?

I can't afford to buy it — Je n'ai pas les moyens de l'acheter

I'd like to pay please — On veut payer, s'il vous plaît

Can I have the bill please? — L'addition, s'il vous plaît

Can I pay by credit card? — Puis-je payer avec une carte de credit?

Do you accept traveller's cheques/Eurocheques/Sterling? — Acceptez-vous les cheques de voyages/Eurocheques/Sterling?

Telephoning

I would like to make a phone call — Je voudrais appeler

I would like Directory Enquiries — Je voudrais les renseignements

I would like to reverse the charges (PCV is pronounced pay say vay) — Je voudrais téléphoner en PCV

Can I speak to...? — Est-ce que je peux parler à ...

I've been cut off — Nous avons été coupés

I can't get through — Je n'arrive pas à obtenir a communication

You may hear:

Ne quittez pas! — I'm trying to connect you, hold the line

Je vous le passe — I'm putting you through

Je suis désolée, mais la ligne est occupée — I'm sorry it's engaged

C'est de la part de qui? — Who's calling

Ce n'est pas le bon numéro — Sorry, wrong number

Transmanche Publicité

Marketing Services

Your **direct** route

to your target market

across the Channel.

If you can handle more

business, talk to us about how

we can get your message

across.

Tel : 00 33 321 96 89 76
Fax: 00 33 321 96 89 76

39 boulevard Jacquard - 62100 Calais

QUICK CURRENCY CONVERTER

FF	£ @ 8.50	£ @ 9.00	£ @ 9.50	FF	£ @ 8.50	£ @ 9.00	£ @ 9.50	FF	£ @ 8.50	£ @ 9.00	£ @ 9.50
1	0.11	0.11	0.10	49	5.76	5.44	5.15	97	11.41	10.77	10.21
2	0.23	0.22	0.21	50	5.88	5.55	5.26	98	11.52	10.88	10.31
3	0.35	0.33	0.31	51	6.00	5.66	5.36	99	11.64	11.00	10.42
4	0.47	0.44	0.42	52	6.11	5.77	5.47	100	11.76	11.11	10.52
5	0.48	0.55	0.52	53	6.23	5.88	5.57	101	11.88	11.22	10.63
6	0.70	0.66	0.63	54	6.35	6.00	5.68	102	12.00	11.33	10.73
7	0.82	0.77	0.73	55	6.47	6.11	5.78	103	12.11	11.44	10.84
8	0.94	0.88	0.84	56	6.58	6.22	5.89	104	12.23	11.55	10.94
9	1.05	1.00	0.97	57	6.70	6.33	6.00	105	12.35	11.66	11.05
10	1.17	1.11	1.05	58	6.82	6.44	6.10	106	12.47	11.77	11.15
11	1.29	1.22	1.15	59	6.94	6.55	6.21	107	12.50	11.88	11.26
12	1.33	1.33	1.26	60	7.05	6.66	6.31	108	12.70	12.00	11.36
13	1.44	1.44	1.36	61	7.17	6.77	6.42	109	12.82	12.11	11.47
14	1.64	1.55	1.47	62	7.29	6.88	6.52	110	12.94	12.22	11.57
15	1.76	1.66	1.57	63	7.41	7.00	6.63	111	13.05	12.33	11.68
16	1.88	1.77	1.68	64	7.52	7.11	6.73	112	13.17	12.44	11.78
17	2.00	1.88	1.78	65	7.64	7.22	6.84	113	13.29	12.55	11.89
18	2.11	2.00	1.89	66	7.76	7.33	6.94	114	13.41	12.66	12.00
19	2.23	2.11	2.00	67	7.88	7.44	7.05	115	13.52	12.77	12.10
20	2.22	2.35	2.10	68	8.00	7.55	7.15	116	13.64	12.88	12.21
21	2.47	2.47	2.21	69	8.11	7.66	7.26	117	13.76	13.00	12.31
22	2.58	2.44	2.31	70	8.23	7.77	7.36	118	13.88	13.11	12.42
23	2.70	2.55	2.42	71	8.35	7.88	7.47	119	14.00	13.22	12.52
24	2.82	2.66	2.52	72	8.47	8.00	7.57	120	14.11	13.33	12.63
25	2.94	2.77	2.63	73	8.58	8.11	7.68	121	14.23	13.44	12.73
26	3.05	2.88	2.73	74	8.70	8.22	7.78	122	14.35	13.55	12.84
27	3.17	3.00	2.84	75	8.82	8.33	7.89	123	14.47	13.66	12.94
28	3.29	3.11	2.94	76	8.94	8.44	8.00	124	14.58	13.77	13.05
29	3.41	3.22	3.05	77	9.05	8.55	8.10	125	14.70	13.88	13.15
30	3.52	3.33	3.15	78	9.17	8.66	8.21	126	14.82	14.00	13.26
31	3.64	3.44	3.26	79	9.29	8.77	8.31	127	14.94	14.11	13.36
32	3.76	3.55	3.36	80	9.41	8.88	8.42	128	15.05	14.22	13.47
33	3.88	3.66	3.47	81	9.52	9.00	8.52	129	15.17	14.33	13.57
34	4.00	3.77	3.57	82	9.64	9.11	8.63	130	15.29	14.44	13.68
35	4.11	3.88	3.68	83	9.76	9.22	8.73	131	15.41	14.55	13.78
36	4.23	4.00	3.78	84	9.88	9.33	8.84	132	15.52	14.66	13.89
37	4.35	4.11	3.89	85	10.00	9.44	8.94	133	15.64	14.77	14.00
38	4.47	4.22	4.00	86	10.11	9.55	9.05	134	15.76	14.88	14.10
39	4.58	4.33	4.10	87	10.23	9.66	9.15	135	15.88	15.00	14.21
40	4.70	4.44	4.21	88	10.35	9.77	9.26	136	16.00	15.11	14.31
41	4.82	4.55	4.31	89	10.47	9.88	9.36	137	16.11	15.22	14.42
42	4.94	4.66	4.42	90	10.58	10.00	9.47	138	16.23	15.33	14.52
43	5.05	4.77	4.52	91	10.70	10.11	9.57	139	16.35	15.44	14.63
44	5.17	4.88	4.63	92	10.82	10.22	9.68	140	16.47	15.55	14.73
45	5.29	5.00	4.73	93	10.94	10.33	9.78	145	17.05	16.11	15.26
46	5.41	5.11	4.84	94	11.05	10.44	9.89	150	17.64	16.66	15.78
47	5.52	5.22	4.94	95	11.17	10.55	10.00	175	20.58	19.44	18.42
48	5.64	5.33	5.05	96	11.29	10.66	10.10	200	23.52	22.22	21.05